# Flossie's Favorites

Copyright 1992 by Kathy Arute

Printed by Delmar Printing Co.
Charlotte, NC

*Cover photo credit:*
Winston-Salem Journal photo by Cookie Snyder

ISBN 0-9632043-0-0

# Contents

**Dedication/Thoughts of Flossie** ... ii
**Meats and Main Dishes** ... 1
    Beef ... 2
    Hamburger ... 4
    Pork ... 13
    Chicken ... 18
    Turkey ... 27
    Seafood ... 28
    Dried Beans ... 29
    Eggs ... 31

**Salads** ... 32
    Vegetable Salads ... 33
    Bean and Pasta ... 37
    Crab and Chicken ... 38
    Molded Salads ... 39
    Fruit Salads ... 45
    Salad Dressing ... 47

**Vegetables** ... 48
    Asparagus ... 49
    Broccoli ... 50
    Cabbage ... 55
    Carrots ... 56
    Corn ... 57
    Mushrooms ... 57
    Onions ... 58
    Potatoes ... 59
    Spinach ... 63
    Squash ... 64
    Tomatoes ... 66
    Vegetable Casseroles ... 66

**Punch** ... 69
**Breads, Pasta and Rice** ... 73
**Cakes, Pies, Cookies** ... 82
    Cakes ... 83
    Pies ... 109
    Cookies ... 123

**Desserts** ... 125
**Candy and Jelly** ... 136
**Appetizers** ... 139
    Dips and Spreads ... 140
    Cheese Appetizers ... 145
    Pickles ... 149

**Index** ... 152

***Special thanks to my dear friends and family who have contributed recipes, encouragements, laughter, friendship and love.***

Audrey Absher
Janice Andrews
Kathy Arute
Shirley Baroody
Libby Barker
Shirley Blackburn
Beth Boyd
Susan Brewer
Jill Brown
Bobbie Burke
Carole Byrd
Kay A. Call
Barbara Chambers
Jo Cheek
Sue Christenbury
Cordie Clark
Frances Clark
Hope Combs
Minnie Cornatzer's
Faye Curry
Diane Doss
Nancy Edwards
Nancy Finger
Betty Jane France

Sheree Garvin
Cookie Greene
Judy Hartman
Gaynell Johnson
Pauline Johnson
Claudine Lovette
Betty Mastin
Jean Mastin
Julie Mastin
Kate Misenheimer
Debbie Montgomery
Ellie McFarland
Gladys McGlamery
Hilda Pardue
Loretta Pfluger
Ardette Seagraves
Ina Seagraves
Mary Seagraves
Bonnie Staley
Della Mae Sparks
Ruth Tucker
Jean Wall
Midge Whittington

*"There's a lot of thanks in giving"*

## A NOTE FROM A FRIEND

"My most pleasant memory of years gone by is one of Flossie Johnson's kitchen. The aroma of country ham and watching Flossie roll out the most delectable biscuits on a crisp autumn morning is a memory to be savored for a lifetime."

—Betty Jane France

"To one of the best cooks and best friends I've ever known. Best wishes and good luck, my precious friend."

—Virg Fox

"Flossie has the gift of hospitality and she expresses love and affection for all of her guests by preparing delicious meals. Darrell, Jessica, and I feel right at home when we sit in the kitchen, laugh, share stories, and savor that delicious food prepared especially for us by Flossie's hands. In return for the joy she has brought into my life, I am happy to see her dream come true in "Flossie's Favorites.""

—Stevie Waltrip

Hi, I'm Flossie Johnson — Junior's Wife. But really I am just me — a country girl who loves life and everybody. My roots are very deep in the country because, you see, I was born to two people who, I think, make up what life is all about. My father and mother were farmers, and also my grandparents. They taught me more about how to live and give than anyone.

My grandmother was one of the wisest women I have had the privilege to know. One thing I will never forget she said, "You do the best you can with what you have." And I sure have put this to good use.

My family consists of two sisters and two brothers. I also had two little brothers who died. We are a very close family. It seems if one of us gets sick, the whole family is ill. Someone once said, "Floss, you have the closest and most loving family of anyone I know," and I had to agree.

I learned to cook when I was just a little girl and had to stand on a chair to reach pots and pans. Mama had to help work in the fields with Daddy and would leave me to cook dinner and look after my younger brother and sister. She would help get everything ready and tell me when to start cooking. We had a wood stove, so I had to start the fire at a certain time in order to get everything ready when it came time for dinner. People in the country ate at 12 noon.

We raised most of our fruits and vegetables and also our hogs, so we had plenty to eat. Most of the time our table was set for at least twelve people for a meal, it doesn't bother me because I was used to it. We had milk cows which provided plenty of fresh milk and butter. I had to churn a lot and I hated that because it took so long. My sister and I had to milk cows every morning before we went to school. We always had to get up early in order to catch the school bus.

I finished school at Wilkesboro High School in 1947. I had wanted to be a nurse and had applied, but a good friend of mine who was a telephone operator talked to me about becoming an operator. It sounded like a good job and lots of fun. So, I went to work in Winsten-Salem, North Carolina, at Southern Bell.

In the meantime, I had met Junior Johnson when I was thirteen and he was twelve. We used to ride the bus to the movies on Saturday night. We would sit in the balcony and he would sit behind me, flip my hair or whisper in my ear. I didn't fall in love with him at first, but after a while it became love and has been ever since. He has been my whole life and I feel like I have been his wife forever.

Everyone has read the stories about Junior and his growing up in the moonshine business. Parts of these stories are true and others just make a good story. Both of our families, at one time or another, made the stuff. It was a way of life and there are not many families in Wilkes County that have not been touched by whiskey. They either made it, sold it, or drank it — and maybe for some they did all three.

I have no regrets about that or what happened to Junior during that time, although it was hard on us. I guess Junior's fast driving in the moonshine days is what led him to become a race car driver. He loved speed and fast cars. He had to in order to out-run the law.

In 1956 Junior was caught at a Still helping his dad and he was sent to Chillicothe, Ohio for two years. I went to see Junior every month and never missed one day writing to him, and he wrote to me every time he was allowed to do so.

We loved each other through all of that and when he served his time and came home, I told him that something had to change because that wasn't the way to do it, and nothing good could ever come out of making a living doing something that was wrong. We bought land, built three chicken houses, started raising chickens and Junior kept driving race cars.

I kept working too, and we put everything we both made back into the business. When we had our chicken houses paid for, we decided to go out on a limb and borrow enough money to build our home. It was hard, but we had good support from our families and friends.

Junior got a bulldozer and leased it to the State, so we had extra money coming in. I took it to the bank and made payments on the money we had borrowed and we were able to stay a little bit ahead. We had our house built and moved in it in 1963 — one of the happiest days of my life.

Junior kept driving and doing good. In 1965 he decided to give up driving and become a car owner, and start his own shop. We built a little one-room garage behind our house. Fred and Rex Lovette gave and sold Junior their equipment and Junior added on. Things went real well and Junior hired Bobby Isaac to drive. Herb Nab had come along with Junior and stayed on with us as a mechanic. We had good years and drivers. Mechanics came and went. We built more on to the shops and Junior put everything back into his racing to make it what it is today.

In 1969 Leroy Yarbrough was our driver and we ran a limited amount of races. But what a year we had! If Winston had been paying the million dollars, we would have been the first to win the Triple Crown.

The most memorable race for me was when Leroy won the Daytona 500. Coming out of the 3rd and 4th turns for the checkered flag, he was racing with Charlie Glotzbach and Donnie Allison. Twelve laps to go, Junior brought Leroy in for fresh tires. We had nothing to lose since Donnie was 3rd, 1 lap down. When Leroy went back on to the track, it was like he was shot out of a cannon — gaining second after second. We were all just standing, hoping and praying for a miracle to happen. People in the grandstands were standing and yelling "Come on, Junior." It was like he was driving the car. The TV and news media were all in Charlie and Cotton Owens' pits just waiting for the race to be over — but the checkered flag fell on Leroy. Talk about hustling for them to get where they wanted to be — but it was on! Our whole crew was laughing and crying. Herb Nab was elated. He couldn't even talk. And me — I still cannot talk about it without a lump coming in my throat. We had just lost one of our crew members to leukemia in January and were so saddened from all of that. I guess I have to say I know God had the biggest part in making that happen — at least, that is what I believe.

At Christmas that year, after the racing was over, I went to the bank and while I was waiting to be helped, one of the executives at the bank came over and said, "Flossie, how does it feel to be almost out of debt?" I said, "What do you mean?" "You have one small payment left which will be in January." Talk about happy — but I was! I cried all the way home. I couldn't wait to tell Junior. What a Christmas present that was for the both of us.

After a few years, Ford pulled out of racing and that left things kind of undecided. Junior kept on working, building motors and doing work for different ones.

In 1971, Richard Howard, who owned Charlotte Motor Speedway at that time, called Junior and asked him to build a Chevrolet for a race. Junior told him, "You get me the money, and I will build you a tractor that will sit on the pole and win the race." I couldn't believe what I was hearing. Junior hung up the phone so excited. He started that night calling, trying to get pieces and parts to put together that car. Sure enough, #3 and Charlie Glotzbach did just that and led the race 'til he was involved in a wreck. That #3 Chevrolet was the talk of racing and people came from everywhere to see it run.

Most of you know all the history and stories about Junior. We have had the best race car drivers in the business: Bobby Allison, Cale Yarborough and Darrell Waltrip. They don't get any better than those three. I wonder what kind of career we would have had if Bobby had stayed. It sure was good for one year. Then came Cale Yarborough — three Championships in a row. Something no one else had done. Our eight years with Cale were great. He and Betty Jo have been such good friends and through the years we have remained real close.

In 1981 came Darrell Waltrip and Stevie. Two people I dearly loved and still do. For Darrell, it was getting out of a mess he was in. And for us, it was a new driver, new car, and new crew. What a year we had. The first to win a Championship that celebrated that night in New York at the Waldorf-Astoria. I felt like Cinderella at the ball. Next year, we won the Championship again. I thought things could never change, but they have. We did win another Championship in 1985. The year Bill Elliott won three million dollars. Since then, things have gone good, but it has not been what we were used to. I guess you could say we were spoiled.

We have had Neil Bonnett, Terry Labonte, Geoff Bodine and Sterling Marlin. They have all been real good and I will always love and care what happens to them. From here on, we will wait and see what happens.

Most of you know about the little boy, Brent Kauthen, that came to live with Junior and me in the summers and finally moved in as part of our household. We loved him as our very own but then a terrible accident took his life and a part of me went with him.

My nieces and nephews are very close and I love them all as if they were my very own. They have helped me so much through some of the difficult times of my life. And Junior's family, his sisters and brothers, are very dear to me and my whole family.

And then there are the guys and girls that have worked for us. I feel like they are a part of Junior and me and they have helped make the success here at the Johnson racing shop.

Also, I want to thank my close friends and relatives who encouraged me and shared their recipes with me for this book.

Then there is a young lady who came into my life, Kathy Arute, whom I have loved like my daughter. She is the one who has encouraged me and helped me to put this book together. Although there is a thirty year difference in our ages, we are very close, and it has meant so much to me to have someone like her in my life.

I hope when you read my cookbook and use the recipes, you will be reminded that you were once a little girl and grew up — maybe not from the country — but that some country will rub off on you from this book.

With love and good cooking, from

*Flossie Johnson*

**"To a Friends house, the way is never long"**

# Meats and Main Dishes

*"Sharing a meal means sharing of self. To take time for others is an intimate celebration of life."*

# Beef

### Beef Stew

3 lbs. beef stew, 1" cubes
1 cup sliced carrots
1 cup diced celery
4 cups peeled, cubed potatoes
1 bay leaf
½ teaspoon thyme

3 tablespoons fat
1 cup diced, peeled rutabagas
1 cup peeled, whole small onions
  or diced onions
2 tablespoons minced parsley
Flour (seasoned with salt and pepper)

Coat cubes of beef in seasoned flour. Brown in hot fat in a big, heavy pot such as a Dutch oven. Cover with boiling water. Simmer for 1½ hours. Add carrots, rutabagas, celery, onions, potatoes, bay leaf, parsley and thyme. Simmer 30 minutes longer or until meat and vegetables are done. If desired, thicken with flour blended into cold water to make gravy.

*"Success is never final, and failure is never fatal. It's courage that counts"*

Notes:

# *Meats and Main Dishes* 3

## Peppered Roast

Trim fat from **5 to 6 lb. boneless Rib-Eye Beef Roast.** *Marinate meat the day before* cooking by combining **½ cup coarsely cracked pepper** and **½ teaspoon ground cardamon seed.** Rub over roast and press in with heel of palm. Place in shallow baking dish, then pour the following Sauce Recipe over beef carefully.

**Sauce:**

| | |
|---|---|
| 2 teaspoons tomato paste or | ¾ cup vinegar |
|     4 tablespoons catsup | ½ teaspoon powder |
| 1 teaspoon paprika | 1 cup soy sauce |

For sauce, mix tomato paste, garlic powder and paprika. Gradually add soy sauce and vinegar. Marinate in refrigerator overnight and spoon marinade over meat several times. Remove meat from marinade and let stand at room temperature for 1 hour. Wrap meat in heavy duty foil. Place in shallow pan and roast in slow oven at 350° for 2½ hours for medium rare, and 3 hours for well-done.

Open foil. Ladle out and reserve drippings. Brown roast at 350° while making gravy. Strain pan drippings and skim off excess fat. Add 1 cup of water to 1 cup of meat juices. Bring to boil, taste and add a little marinade if desired. Thicken gravy with **1½ tablespoons cornstarch** mixed with ¼ cup cold water. Heat and stir until smooth. Serve gravy with roast. *(I use rolled rump roast except for very special occasions.)*

**Notes:**

# Hamburger

### Barbecued Meatballs

1 cup bread crumbs
½ cup milk
1 lb. ground beef

1 teaspoon salt
1 teaspoon pepper
1½ tablespoons Worcestershire® Sauce

Shape into 12 meatballs and put into a baking dish.

¼ cup vinegar
1 tablespoon brown sugar
½ cup catsup

½ cup chopped green pepper
½ cup chopped onion
½ cup water

Mix sauce and pour over meatballs. Bake uncovered in 375° oven for 45 minutes to one hour.

### Deluxe Barbecued Meatballs

1½ lb. lean hamburger
1 small onion
1 small green pepper
5 or 6 slices of bread, crumbled

½ cup milk
¼ teaspoon pepper
1 teaspoon salt

Mix ingredients. Make into balls the size of a large egg or smaller. Place into baking pan.

2 tablespoons vinegar
2 cups catsup

2 tablespoons Worcestershire® Sauce
1½ cups water

Mix and pour over meatballs. Bake at 350° for 45 minutes to one hour.

**Notes:**

# *Meats and Main Dishes*

### Beef-A-Roni

1 lb. ground beef
1 large can tomatoes
1 green pepper, diced
1 large onion, chopped
3 cups macaroni

Fry meat, onions and pepper. Drain. Cook macaroni until tender. Add fried ingredients and tomatoes. Simmer over low heat for 20 minutes.

### Bar-B-Q Meatballs

3 lb. hamburger
1½ cups soft bread crumbs
¾ teaspoon pepper
1¼ cups plus 2 tablespoons milk
¾ cup sugar
3 (8 oz) cans tomato sauce
2 med. onions, chopped
1½ teaspoons salt
½ teaspoon chili powder
¾ cup Worcestershire® Sauce
¼ cup plus 2 tablespoons vinegar

Mix together first 7 ingredients. Make into balls. Put in oil and brown. Bring the Worcestershire® Sauce, sugar, vinegar and tomato sauce to a boil. Cook over low heat for 1 minute. Stir occasionally. Pour over meatballs. Bake at 325° for 30 minutes.

### Beef and Bean Casserole

1 lb. ground beef
½ teaspoon salt
1 lb. (12 oz) can Pork & Beans
1 tablespoon Worcestershire® Sauce
1 tablespoon brown sugar
½ cup chopped onion
¼ teaspoon pepper
½ cup catsup
1 tablespoon vinegar
1 green pepper, diced

Brown beef and onion together. Pour off fat. Add remaining ingredients. Mix well. Pour into casserole dish. Bake at 350° for 30 minutes.

## Budget Casserole

1 lb. hamburger
1 onion, chopped
2 cans tomato soup
1 cup grated cheese or 1 can cheddar cheese soup
⅓ cup milk
1 can cream of chicken soup
Grated cheese (for top)
8 oz. egg noodles

Brown hamburger and onion lightly. Add tomato soup and simmer for a few minutes. Cook noodles by package directions. Drain. Add cheese or cheese soup, milk and chicken soup. Mix well. Put layer of noodles in greased 2-quart oblong baking dish. Add meat mixture and cover with remaining noodles. Sprinkle top with grated cheese. Bake in 350° oven until bubbly, about 30 minutes. (I use Cheddar Cheese Soup for this recipe).

## Chili

1 lb. hamburger meat, browned
1 cup brown sugar
2 tablespoons chili powder
1 cup onions, browned
4 small cans tomato sauce
Salt and pepper to taste

Brown meat and onions in a dutch oven. Add remaining ingredients. Simmer for 1 hour, covered. Stir occasionally.

**Notes:**

# Meats and Main Dishes

### Chili Beef Soup

1½ lbs. ground chuck
¼ teaspoon salt
1 tablespoon chopped parsley
1 large can tomatoes, drained
1 env. dry onion soup mix
¼ teaspoon oregano
1 bay leaf

1 can tomato sauce
2 to 3 cups water
Chili powder to taste
Crushed red pepper to taste
Salt and pepper
¼ teaspoon basil
2 tablespoons sugar

Brown chuck. Add all ingredients together. Simmer, covered, for several hours. You may add **"Veg-All"® vegetables** for stew or **"Veg-All"® mixed vegetables** and **red kidney beans.**

### Chili Sauce (For canning)

1½ cups distilled white vinegar
1 inch broken stick cinnamon
5-½ lbs. (22 med.) tomatoes, washed peeled, quartered
1 teaspoon cayenne pepper
¼ teaspoon red pepper

1 teaspoon whole cloves
1 teaspoon celery seed
1 cup granulated sugar
2 tablespoons chopped onion
2 tablespoons salt

Combine vinegar, cloves, cinnamon and celery seed. Bring to a boil. Remove from heat. Set aside. Combine ½ of the tomatoes, ½ cup sugar, onions and cayenne pepper in deep kettle. Boil vigorously, stirring frequently for 30 minutes. Stir in remaining tomatoes and sugar. Boil vigorously, stirring frequently for 30 minutes longer. Strain vinegar and discard spices. Add spiced vinegar and salt to boiling tomato mixture, stirring constantly. Continue boiling for 15 minutes or until desired consistency is reached. Pour immediately into hot, sterilized jars, filling to within ⅛ inch from top. Seal each jar at once. To retain color, wrap jars individually in brown paper before storing.

**Notes:**

## Enchiladas

1 (12 count) pkg. tortillas
1 lb. ground beef (chuck)
1 pkg. Sauer's® chili mix
1 med. chopped onion
1 (8 oz) pkg. mild Cheddar Cheese, grated
1 (15 or 16 oz) can tomato sauce
1 (16 oz) can tomatoes or juice
½ to 1 cup water
1 cup chopped onions

Brown meat. Add onion, chili mix, tomato sauce, tomatoes, and water. Cook over medium heat until tender but juicy, about 15 minutes.

Dip tortillas into chili, one at a time. Put heaping tablespoon meat mixture, 1 teaspoon onion, and 1 teaspoon cheese on tortilla and roll up. Place in large baking dish, 9x12-inch, until all are fixed. Pour remainder chili mixture over this. Sprinkle remainder cheese on top. Heat in oven until cheese is melted, approximately 5-10 minutes in 350° oven.

## Hamburger Casserole

1 lb. hamburger
1 large onion, chopped
1 can tomato soup
1 cup water
Salt and Pepper
1 teaspoon chili powder
½ cup green pepper, chopped
1 cup canned corn or green peas, drained

Brown meat and onion. Add to other ingredients. Put in large casserole dish.

**Topping:** Mix ¾ **cup self-rising corn meal, 1 tablespoon flour, 1 egg,** ½ **cup milk** and **1 tablespoon cooking oil.** Mix and drop by teaspoons over ingredients in casserole dish. Bake 25-30 minutes at 350° until brown on top.

**Notes:**

# Meats and Main Dishes

## Hamburger Pie Casserole

1 medium onion, chopped
1 lb. ground beef
¾ teaspoon salt
Dash pepper
1 lb. can (2 cups) cut green beans, drained, or ½ lb. green beans cooked and drained
1 can condensed tomato soup
5 medium potatoes, cooked or use instant potatoes
½ cup warm milk
1 beaten egg
Salt and Pepper
½ cup shredded cheese (optional)

Cook onion in small amount of hot fat until tender but not brown. Add meat and seasonings. Brown slightly and add drained beans and soup. Pour into greased, 1½ quart casserole. Mash potatoes and while hot, add eggs and milk with seasonings. Drop in mounds over meat. If you like, sprinkle ½ cup shredded cheese over top. Bake 25-30 minutes in 350° oven.

## Hamburger Stuff

1½ lb. ground chuck
1 tablespoon catsup
½ teaspoon salt
1 (10 oz) can beef bouillon
⅓ cup sour cream
2 tablespoons minced onion or ½ cup chopped onion
1 tablespoon parsley flakes
1 can cream of mushroom soup
1 (4 oz) can sliced mushroom

Brown beef and onions and drain excess fat. Mix together remaining ingredients except mushroom soup and sour cream. Simmer until meat is done, then add soup and sour cream. Serve over rice and noodles.

**Notes:**

## Juicy Meat Loaf

2 lbs. ground beef
1 1/3 cups evaporate milk
2/3 cup rolled oats*
1/4 cup finely cut onions
1/2 to 2/3 cup finely cut celery
1/2 cup finely cut bell peppers
2/3 cup tomato catsup
2 teaspoons salt
1/2 teaspoon pepper
2-3 bacon slices, cut in half

Mix thoroughly. Shape into loaf. Put into greased pan. Put bacon on top, and bake at 350° for 1 1/2 hours. Baste occasionally. Serve hot or cold. *Soft bread crumbs can replace oats if amounts are increased to 1 cup.

## Lasagna

1 lb. ground beef
3/4 cup onion
1/2 garlic clove
1 tablespoon parsley
1/2 teaspoon oregano
1/2 teaspoon salt
Dash of pepper
1 cup (8 oz) cottage cheese
1 egg
1/4 cup Parmesan cheese
2 cans crescent rolls
2 slices Mozzarella cheese
1 tablespoon milk
1 tablespoon sesame seeds
1 can tomato sauce

Cook ground beef, onion, garlic, parsley, oregano, salt and pepper. Add tomato sauce. Mix cottage cheese, egg, Parmesan cheese. Arrange Crescent rolls on cookie sheet by taking 2 triangles and patting into one large rectangle. Spread 1/2 ground beef mixture on 1/2 of rolled dough rectangle. Put cottage cheese mix on top of ground beef. Continue with another layer (rest of beef mixture) on cottage cheese mix. Put Mozzarella slices on top. Lap over half of rectangle. Seal edges. Brush milk on top of crust. Sprinkle sesame seeds on top. Cook at 375° for 20-25 minutes.

Notes:

# Meats and Main Dishes

## Meatballs

1½ lbs. ground beef  
½ (8 oz) can tomato sauce (Reserve other half of tomato sauce)  
Salt and pepper to taste  
1 onion  
1 egg

Combine ingredients and form balls. Place in pan. Mix the other half of tomato sauce with **1 tomato sauce can of water, 2 teaspoons mustard, 2 tablespoons brown sugar,** and **¼ cup vinegar.** Combine and pour over meatballs. Bake 1 hour at 350°.

## Stuffed Peppers

6 med. green peppers  
1 lb. ground beef  
2 cups stewed tomatoes  
2 tablespoons Worcestershire® sauce  
1 cup shredded sharp process American Cheese  
1 large onion  
1 tablespoon fat  
¾ cup pkg. rice  
Salt and pepper

Cut tops off green peppers. Remove seeds and membranes. Pre-cook pepper in boiling salted water about 5 minutes. Drain. Sprinkle inside with salt. Brown meat and onions in hot fat. Add tomatoes, rice, Worcestershire® sauce, salt and pepper to taste. Cover and simmer about 5 minutes until rice is almost tender. Add cheese. Stuff peppers, stand upright in 10x6" baking dish. Bake uncovered in moderate oven 350° for 25 minutes. Sprinkle tops with additional shredded cheese.

**Notes:**

## Jean's Stuffed Green Peppers

4 green peppers  
2 tablespoons margarine  
3 tablespoons chopped onion  
½ lb. ground beef  
1 (#303) can tomatoes  
1 cup cooked rice  

⅛ teaspoon paprika  
¼ teaspoon celery seed  
½ teaspoon Worcestershire® sauce  
½ teaspoon salt  
½ cup shredded cheese  

Take centers out of peppers. Scald green peppers in boiling water. Set in shallow pan with a little water or tomato juice. Cook beef and drain. Add other ingredients, except cheese, and simmer for a few minutes. Stuff peppers and sprinkle with cheese. Bake in a 350° oven until bubbly hot for 30 minutes.

## Texas Hash

2 tablespoons fat in pan  
1 green pepper, chopped  

1 or 2 onions, chopped  
1 lb. ground beef  

Brown above ingredients. Add:

1 cup tomatoes  
1 teaspoon chili powder  
Dash of pepper  

1 cup Minute Rice®  
2½ teaspoon salt  

Pour into baking dish. Cover with foil. Bake at 350° for 30 minutes or longer.

Notes:

# Pork

### Black-Eyed Peas and Sausage
#### Great for New Years!

1 (8 oz) bacon, diced
1 green pepper, chopped
1 clove garlic, minced
1 (15 oz) can warm water
½ teaspoon salt
1 tomato, peeled and diced

2 cups celery, chopped
1 cup onion, chopped
3 (15 oz) cans black-eyed peas
   and liquid
¼ teaspoon cayenne pepper (optional)
1 lb. smoked sausage, thinly sliced

Fry bacon. Drain grease, leaving 2 tablespoons in pan. Add celery, green pepper, onion and garlic to the bacon drippings and saute until onion is clear. Transfer to Dutch oven and add peas, water, salt, pepper and tomato. While bringing peas to a boil, fry sausage and drain well. Add sausage to peas and simmer 40 minutes or until desired thickness of broth.

### Breakfast Casserole

1 lb. sausage, browned and drained
1 pkg. croutons (unseasoned)
1 cup cheddar cheese, grated

6 eggs, well-beaten
1 cup milk

Grease 13x9x2-inch casserole dish. Place croutons in bottom of pan. Add sausage. Sprinkle cheese over sausage. Combine milk and eggs. Pour over sausage. Let set in refrigerator 2 hours or longer. Bake at 350° for 35-40 minutes.

Notes:

## Brunch Casserole

1 lb. bulk pork sausage
1 (8 oz) can refrigerated crescent dinner rolls
2 cups (8 oz) shredded mozzarella cheese
4 eggs, beaten
¾ cup milk
¼ teaspoon salt
⅛ teaspoon pepper

Crumble sausage in a medium skillet. Cook over medium heat until brown, stirring occasionally. Drain well. Line bottom of a buttered 9x13x2-inch baking dish with crescent rolls, firmly pressing perforations to seal. Sprinkle with the sausage and cheese.

Combine remaining ingredients. Beat well and pour over sausage. Bake at 425° for 15 minutes or until set. Let stand 15 minutes. Cut into squares and serve immediately.

## Ham and Cauliflower Casserole

2½-3 cups cooked cauliflower
1 can cream of celery soup
½ cup milk
1 cup ham, cooked and diced
Buttered bread crumbs

Mix soup and milk. Pour over cooked cauliflower. Add diced ham and mix lightly. Pour into casserole. Sprinkle bread crumbs on top. Bake ½ hour at 375°.

## Macaroni and Tomatoes

2 cups uncooked macaroni
1 lb. sausage, cooked, browned, drained
1 quart can of tomatoes, cut up fine

Cook macaroni by package directions. Salt and pepper to taste. Mix macaroni, tomatoes, and sausage. Pour into casserole dish. Bake for 40 minutes at 400°.

# Meats and Main Dishes

## Ham and Cheese Sandwiches

2 pkgs. dinner rolls
6 oz. swiss cheese

6 oz. sliced ham

Cut rolls lengthwise. Layer with ham and cheese. Mix:

1 stick margarine (melted)
1½ tablespoon mustard

1½ tablespoon poppy seed
½ teaspoon Worcestershire® sauce

Pour mixture over rolls. Let stand several hours or overnight in refrigerator. Bake 15 minutes at 350°.

## Ham and Swiss Cheese Biscuits

3 pkgs. pull-apart rolls
6 tablespoons hot mustard
1 tablespoon poppy seeds
Swiss Cheese

Ham, thinly sliced
2 tablespoons minced onion
2 sticks melted margarine

Mix mustard, poppy seeds, onion and margarine. Cut pull-apart rolls in half. Spread mustard mixture over bottom half of rolls. Layer with ham and cheese. Put top back on rolls. Cook in 300° oven for 20 minutes.

Notes:

## Raisin Sauce For Ham
*"Will make any ham taste special"*

1 cup raisins  
¾ cup brown sugar  
¼ teaspoon salt  
5 cloves  
¼ teaspoon Worcestershire® sauce  

1 cup water  
1 teaspoon cornstarch  
Pinch of pepper  
1 tablespoon vinegar  

Cover raisins with water. Simmer for 10 minutes. Mix sugar, cornstarch, salt and pepper. Add to raisins. Cook until slightly thickened and add remaining ingredients, blending thoroughly.

## Sausage Balls

1 lb. hot sausage  
2½ cups grated extra sharp cheddar cheese  

2¼ cups Bisquick®  
¼ teaspoon salt  

Mix with hands. Shape into balls. Bake at 350° for 20 minutes.

## Sausage Casserole

*Layer the following in a casserole dish:*

8 slices bread, cubed  
2 cups grated Cheddar cheese  

1 lb. sausage, fried and drained  

Set aside. Now mix **4 eggs, ²/₄ teaspoon dry mustard,** and **2½ cups milk** together. Pour over layers in casserole dish. Now mix **1 can cream of mushroom soup,** ½ **cup milk** and ½ **teaspoon salt.** Pour over layers. Cover and refrigerate overnight. Bake at 375° for one hour.

# Meats and Main Dishes

## Sausage Pinwheels

1 lb. sausage
2 cups plain flour
2 teaspoons baking powder
2 tablespoons sugar
¼ teaspoon salt
⅓ cup shortening
⅔ cup milk

Mix and sift together dry ingredients. Cut in shortening. Add ¾ cup milk. Knead on a floured surface. Roll out to ⅛-inch thick rectangle. Spread sausage over this. Roll up from the long side. Slice into about ¼-inch slices. Bake at 400° for 20 to 25 minutes.

## Special Occasion Sausage and Eggs

1½ lb. sausage
1 stick butter
2 cups shredded Longhorn cheese
2½ cups half and half
1½ teaspoons dry mustard
9 slices white bread with crusts removed
8 eggs
1½ teaspoon salt

Cook sausage over low heat until done and a crumbly consistency. Drain and set aside. Spread butter on bread and cut in cubes. Place cubes in 9x13-inch Pyrex® dish. Sprinkle sausage on bread and cheese on top of sausage. Combine remaining ingredients. Beat well and pour over cheese. Chill 8 hours or overnight. Bake at 350° for 40-50 minutes until brown.

Notes:

## Stuffed Pork Chops

Have pork chops cut 1-inch thick, split, and filled with the following:

2 cups soft bread crumbs
2 eggs
1/4 cup finely cut celery

1 teaspoon salt
1/8 teaspoon red pepper
1/4 cup melted butter

Place in a pan and bake at 400° for 45 minutes and then turn oven to 350° for one additional hour.

# Chicken

## Baked Chicken Breast

8 boned and skinned chicken breasts
1/2 pt. light sour cream

1 small jar chipped beef
1 can cream of chicken soup

Spray baking dish with Pam®. Place chipped beef on bottom of pan. Put chicken on top. Top with mixture of soup and sour cream. Do not salt chicken. Cook 3 hours on 300°. Cover for first 2 hours.

*"We keep the best of that which we give away"*

Notes:

## Chicken-Asparagus Casserole

2 (15 oz) cans asparagus, drained
3/4 cup sliced almonds, toasted
1 (10-3/4 oz) can cream of celery soup, undiluted
1/2 cup Chablis or other dry white wine
1 (8 oz) can sliced water chestnuts, drained
3 1/2 cups diced cooked chicken
3/4 cup mayonnaise
1 (5/3 oz) can evaporated milk
1/4 cup grated Parmesan cheese

Layer asparagus, water chestnuts, almonds, and chicken in a lightly greased, 12x8x2-inch baking dish. Combine soup, mayonnaise, wine and milk. Mix well. Spoon mixture over chicken, and sprinkle with cheese. Bake at 350° for 20 minutes.

## Flossie's Chicken Casserole

4 chicken breasts
1 can cream of celery soup
1 can cream of chicken soup
1 small can evaporated milk
3/4 cup chicken broth
1 small pkg. Pepperidge Farm® cornbread stuffing mix
1 stick margarine

Stew chicken breasts. Let cool. Remove bones and skin. Cut into chunks. Add soups, milk, broth and mix well. Melt margarine and mix with stuffing. Put a layer about half of mixture into bottom of 9x12-inch pan. Add chicken mixture and top with remaining stuffing mixture. Bake at 350° for about 30 minutes or until top is brown.

**Notes:**

### Delicious Chicken Casserole

| | |
|---|---|
| 1 (3 lb) chicken | 1 stick margarine |
| 8 oz. sour cream | 1 cup cream of mushroom soup |
| 2 cups chicken broth | 1 cup cream of celery soup |
| 1 (8 oz) pkg. herb seasoning dressing | |

Cook and debone chicken. Cut into cubes and put in bottom of a 9x12-inch greased baking dish. Mix the sour cream and undiluted soups together and spread over chicken. Melt the margarine and mix in the dressing mix and broth. Spread this over the top of the casserole and bake uncovered at 350° for 30 minutes.

### Jean's Chicken Casserole

| | |
|---|---|
| 8 slices day-old bread | ½ teaspoon salt |
| 2 cups cooked chicken, diced | ½ cup grated cheese |
| ¼ cup chopped onion | 2 eggs, slightly beaten |
| ½ cup chopped green pepper | 1½ cups milk |
| ½ cup chopped celery | 1 can cream of chicken soup |
| ½ cup mayonnaise | |

Butter 2 slices bread and cut in ½-inch cubes. Set aside. Cut remaining bread into 1-inch cubes. Place ½ of 1-inch cubes in buttered baking dish. Combine chicken, vegetables, mayonnaise, and salt. Spread over bread cubes. Sprinkle remaining unbuttered cubes over mixture. Sprinkle on cheese. Combine eggs and milk and pour over all. Cover and chill for 1 hour or longer. Spoon soup over top. Sprinkle with buttered cubes and bake for 1 hour at 325°.

Notes:

# Meats and Main Dishes

### Brenda's Chicken Casserole

1 med. chicken, boiled, deboned and diced*
1 can cream of chicken soup*
1 can cream of celery soup*
1 cup milk*

1 stick butter or margarine
1 pkg. Pepperidge Farm® Dressing Mix
1½ cups chicken broth
1 medium onion, chopped

Mix first four ingredients*. Place in casserole dish. In separate bowl, mix together remaining ingredients. Pour mixture over chicken in casserole dish. Bake at 350° for 30 minutes.

### Betty's Chicken Casserole

4 to 6 chicken breasts
1 cup sour cream
3 teaspoons poppy seed
1½ rolls Ritz® crackers

2 cans cream of chicken soup
1 cup chicken broth, if desired
1½ sticks margarine, melted

Cook chicken breasts until tender and season to taste with salt and pepper. Mix soup, broth, sour cream, and poppy seed. Remove chicken from bone and place in 9x13-inch pan. Pour soup mixture over chicken. Crush crackers and mix with melted margarine, and sprinkle over chicken and soup mixture. Bake at 350° for 40-45 minutes.

*"The best gifts are those tied with heart strings"*

Notes:

## Chicken Imperial

6 chicken breasts
1 cup sherry
1 cup bread crumbs
1 teaspoon salt
¼ teaspoon freshly ground pepper
2 tablespoons parsley

1 clove of garlic, crushed
1 cup chopped or slivered almonds, divided
¾ cup melted butter or margarine
1 cup grated Parmesan cheese

Marinate chicken in sherry (Taylor New York Golden Sherry®) for 2 to 3 hours. Pat dry with paper towel. Combine bread crumbs, salt, pepper, Parmesan cheese, parsley, garlic, and ¾ cup almonds. Dip chicken in butter. Roll in bread crumbs mixture. Arrange in a 9x13x2-inch pan and sprinkle with remaining almonds. Bake at 350° for 1 hour.

## Chicken Pie

4 chicken breasts
1 medium onion
2 cups chicken broth

2-3 stalks of celery
1 can cream of chicken soup

Cook chicken until tender in celery and onion. Arrange chicken in a large baking dish. Bring to a boil, cream of chicken soup and chicken broth. Pour over chicken pieces.

**Make a batter of:**

1 stick melted margarine
1 cup self-rising flour

½ teaspoon black pepper
1 cup buttermilk

Pour batter over chicken pieces and broth mix. Bake at 425° for 25-30 minutes.

**Notes:**

## Chicken Salad

1 large chicken, cooked & diced
1 pt. mayonnaise (Hellman's)®
1 pt. sweet salad cubes
5 boiled eggs, diced
2 cups celery, chopped

Mix ingredients together when all is cool.

## Chicken Spectacular

3 cups cooked chicken, diced
1 med. jar diced pimento
1 cup mayonnaise
1 can sliced water chestnuts
Salt and Pepper
1 box Uncle Ben's® long grain and wild rice
1 can French-style green beans, drained
1 can cream of celery soup

Mix ingredients and put in casserole. Top with **Pepperidge Farm® stuffing mix.** Bake at 350° for 25-30 minutes.

## Chicken Supreme

2 cups cooked, cubed chicken
2 tablespoons chopped green olives
¾ cup chopped celery
½ cup slivered almonds
2 tablespoons sliced ripe olives
2 tablespoons mixed sweet pickle relish
2 hard boiled eggs (sliced)
¾ cup mayonnaise
Salt and pepper to taste

Mix ingredients and serve.

**Notes:**

## Creamy Baked Chicken Breasts

4 whole chicken breasts, split, skinned and boned
¼ cup dry white wine
1 cup herb-seasoned stuffing mix, crushed
8 (4x4") slices Swiss cheese
1 (10-¾ oz) can cream of chicken soup, undiluted
¼ cup margarine, melted

Arrange chicken in a lightly greased 9x13x2-inch baking dish. Top with cheese slices. Combine soup and wine, stirring well. Spoon sauce evenly over chicken and sprinkle with stuffing mix. Drizzle butter over crumbs. Bake at 350° for 45 to 55 minutes.

## Easy Chicken Pie

1 unbaked pie shell
¾ cup cooked chopped chicken
1 can cream of chicken soup
½ cup melted margarine
1 (16 oz) mixed vegetables drained, canned or frozen
1¼ cups Ritz® cracker crumbs

Bake pie shell until lightly brown. Combine drained vegetables, chicken and soup. Mix well. Spoon into pie shell. Toss cracker crumbs in bowl with butter. Sprinkle over pie. Bake at 350° for 40 minutes.

Notes:

## Green Chili Chicken Casserole

Boil **1 chicken or 4 chicken breasts** until done. Take meat from bone.

½ can chicken broth
1 can Cream of Mushroom soup
1 onion, chopped
1½ cups Monterey Jack cheese, grated

1 can Cream of Chicken soup
1 small can green chilies, chopped
1 pkg. tortillas (corn is best)
   (will be in case with biscuits)

Sauté onion in a little oil. Warm together soups, broth, chopped chilies, and onion. In large casserole dish, make layers of tortillas, chicken, soup mixtures and cheese — always ending with cheese. Bake at 300° for 20-30 minutes.

## Melt In Your Mouth Chicken Pie

2½ to 3 lb. fryer
1 can undiluted cream of mushroom
   or cream of chicken soup
½ teaspoon black pepper
1 cup buttermilk

2 cups reserved chicken broth
1 stick margarine, melted
1 cup self-rising flour
1 teaspoon salt

Cook chicken until tender (pressure cooker speeds time). Remove meat from bones. Reserve broth. Cut chicken into small pieces and place in 9x13x2-inch pan. In a saucepan, mix and bring to a boil the reserved chicken broth and soup. In another bowl, combine margarine, pepper, salt, flour and buttermilk. Mix thoroughly to form batter. Pour broth mixture over chicken. Spoon batter over top. Bake at 425° for 25 to 30 minutes.

**Notes:**

## Oven Barbecued Chicken

1²/₃ lb. dressed chicken. Brown in fat. Meanwhile, make sauce of the following:

1 cup ketchup
2 tablespoons brown sugar
½ tablespoon prepared mustard
½ cup chopped celery
1 med. onion, chopped
2 tablespoons vinegar

¼ cup lemon juice
3 tablespoons Worcestershire® sauce
1 cup water
2 teaspoons salt
¼ teaspoon Tabasco® Sauce

Combine ingredients and simmer for 10 minutes. Place browned pieces of chicken in baking dish. Pour sauce over chicken. Bake, uncovered, at 350° for one hour, basting frequently. Test drumsticks for doneness and if pink meat shows, bake for 15 minutes more.

## Poppy Seed Chicken
(Delicious over rice or pasta noodles!)

3 cups cooked chicken
8 oz. sour cream
1½ cups crumbled Ritz® crackers

1 can cream of chicken soup
1 stick melted margarine
1 tablespoon poppy seed

Put chicken in bottom of baking dish. Blend soup and sour cream together and pour over chicken. Combine margarine, crumbs and poppy seed. Sprinkle on top. Bake at 350° for 30 minutes.

**Notes:**

*Meats and Main Dishes*

# Turkey

### Crunchy Turkey Casserole

3 cups cooked, diced turkey
   (chicken may also be used)
1 cup cooked rice
1 can sliced water chestnuts, drained
1 cup celery, diced
2 tablespoons onion, chopped
½ cup almonds, sliced (optional)
1 can cream of chicken soup
   (undiluted)
½ cup mayonnaise
½-¾ cup Corn Flakes® or Rice
   Krispies,® crushed

Combine ingredients except Corn Flakes® or Rice Krispies.® Mix well. Bake at 350° for 45 minutes. Last 15 minutes, add Corn Flake® crumbs or Rice Krispies.®

### Turkey Tetrazzini
(Chicken, tuna, or beef may be used in place of turkey)

1 lb. spaghetti noodles
1½ cups diced celery
1 cups diced green pepper
¼ cup onion, chopped
½ lb. mushrooms, canned or fresh
   (1 can mushroom soup okay)
¾ cup butter or margarine
¼ cup flour
2 cups milk
½ lb. sharp cheese
¼ teaspoon pepper
2 teaspoons salt
2 tablespoons Worcestershire® Sauce
1½ cups diced, cooked turkey
¾ cup Parmesan cheese

Cook spaghetti according to package instructions. Prepare sauce: Cook celery, green pepper, onion and mushrooms in the butter until onion is just transparent. Add flour and blend well. Add milk all at once, stirring constantly until uniformly thickened. Blend in cheese, salt, pepper, Worcestershire®, turkey, stirring until cheese melts. Serve over hot spaghetti. Sprinkle Parmesan cheese on top. *Option:* place in 13x9x2-inch pan and put in 350° oven for 20 minutes.

Notes:

# Seafood

## Shrimp Marguerite

4 lbs. shrimp, cooked
5 tablespoons salad oil
1/4 cup chopped green pepper
1 1/2 teaspoons salt
1/2 teaspoon mace
2 cans tomato soup, undiluted
2 cups cooked rice

3 tablespoons lemon juice
1/2 cup chopped onion
3 tablespoons butter
1/2 teaspoon pepper
Dash cayenne pepper
2 cups sour cream
1/2 cup white wine

Marinate shrimp in lemon juice and oil for 2 hours. Drain. Saute onion and peppers in butter. Add all ingredients. Mix well and pour into greased 2-qt. casserole dish. May top with a little **paprika** and **slivered almonds**. Bake at 350° for 45 minutes to 1 hour. May mix and refrigerate overnight to improve flavor.

## Tuna Surprise

2 tablespoons margarine
1 cup onion, cut up, not too fine

1 cup celery, cut up, not too fine

Cook ingredients until tender. Do not overcook. Add the following:

2 tablespoons water
1 small can tuna, rinsed, drained
1 pkg. (5 1/2 oz) cashew nuts, rinsed to remove salt

1 can cream of mushroom soup, undiluted

Serve over **Chow Mein®  noodles**.

Notes:

# Dried Beans

### 3 Bean Casserole

1 lb. can kidney beans, drained
1 lb. can lima beans, drained
1 lb. can pork & beans, not drained
¼ cup vinegar
½ cup brown sugar
1 teaspoon mustard
¼ cup barbecue sauce
¼ cup catsup
1 med. onion, chopped

Mix ingredients and bake for 1 hour, uncovered, at 350°.

### 3 Bean Hot Dish

5 slices bacon, diced
1 lb. hamburger
1 med. onion, diced
½ cup brown sugar
¾ cup ketchup
2½ cups lima beans, drained
1 (16 oz) can kidney beans, drained
1 (16 oz) can pork and beans
1 tablespoon Worcestershire® sauce

Put bacon, hamburger, and onion in skillet. Cook until brown. Drain. Mix brown sugar, ketchup and Worcestershire® sauce. Add to meat mixture. Combine with lima beans, kidney beans, and pork and beans. Put into a 9x13-inch baking dish. Bake for 1 hour at 350°.

Notes:

## Baked Beans

2 (16 oz) cans of pork and beans
1 large apple, chopped
¼ cup raisins
½ cup chopped onion
¾ cup firmly-packed brown sugar

½ cup sweet relish
1 tablespoon prepared mustard
¾ cup catsup
4 strips bacon, fried and crumbled

Combine ingredients. Bake, covered at 250° for 1½ hours.

## Butter Bean Casserole

2 pkgs. frozen butter beans
1 cup chopped onions
1 cup cheddar cheese
¼ cup melted butter
2 cans cream of chicken soup, undiluted

1 cup sliced carrots
¼ cup chopped celery
2 cups bread crumbs
2 cans cream of mushroom soup, undiluted

Cook butter beans according to package directions. Drain. Cook carrots, onions, and celery until tender. Drain. Add all ingredients together, *leaving out* cheese, bread crumbs and butter. Put in casserole dish. Now mix together cheese, melted butter and bread crumbs. Sprinkle over casserole. Bake at 375° for 15 minutes.

Notes:

*Meats and Main Dishes*

# Eggs

### Kid's Favorite Cadillac Egg Omelet

2 eggs, beaten
4-6 crackers, crushed
2 tablespoons milk

Salt and pepper to taste
1 slice cheese (optional)

Mix ingredients. Fry in well greased pan.

Notes:

# Salads

*"It's what you learn after you know it all that counts"*

# Vegetable Salads

### Barbecue Slaw

1 gal. grated cabbage
1 cup vinegar
1 tablespoon salt
1 jar small pimento
1 teaspoon Texas Pete® hot sauce
1 (20 oz) ketchup
1 cup sugar
1 pt. sweet pickles
½ teaspoon black pepper

Mix together and put in a glass jar. *Keep in refrigerator for six months.*

### Best Cole Slaw

1 small head cabbage, shredded
1 medium green pepper, chopped
½ cup salad oil
½ cup vinegar
¼ cup sugar
1 teaspoon salt

Combine all ingredients. Let stand in refrigerator 3 hours before serving.

*"Life is like an onion — you peel off one layer at a time, and sometimes you weep"*

**Notes:**

### Green Pea Salad

1 (17 oz) can green peas, drained
½ cup pimento
¼ cup mayonnaise
Pimento strips

3 hard-cooked eggs, chopped
½ cup sweet pickle, chopped
¼ teaspoon celery seeds
Lettuce leaves

Combine peas, eggs, pickle, pimento, celery seeds and mayonnaise. Mix well and chill. Serve on lettuce leaves. Garnish salad with pimento strips.

### Marinated Slaw

1 large cabbage, shredded
1 green pepper, diced
2 onions, chopped
2 cups sugar
1 tablespoon plus 1 teaspoon sugar

¾ cup Mazola® oil
1 teaspoon celery seed
1 cup vinegar
1 teaspoon dry mustard
1 tablespoon salt

Combine in large bowl first four ingredients. Bring the next six ingredients to a boil. Pour over cabbage mixture. Seal. Do not stir for four hours. Keeps a long time in refrigerator.

### Vegetable Salad

1 can green peas, drained
1 can pimento, sliced
1 small onion, diced
1 bell pepper, sliced

2 cans french green beans, drained
4 stalks celery, diced
Salt

Combine above ingredients. Make a dressing of **1 cup sugar, 1 teaspoon paprika,** and **½ cup salad oil.** Blend and pour over salad. Let stand overnight.

**Notes:**

# Salads

### Wilted Lettuce

1 large bunch of lettuce  
4 slices of bacon (save bacon fat)  
4 to 6 green onions  
1 teaspoon vinegar

Wash lettuce and drain well. Cup up fine. Slice onions on top, add vinegar and crumbled bacon. Heat bacon fat until hot. Pour over lettuce and onions and serve.

## Bean and Pasta

### Amish Macaroni Salad

1½ cups macaroni, cooked and drained  
6 hard boiled eggs  
Onions, celery, carrots, parsley and pimento to taste

Mix above ingredients. *Dressing:* **1½ cups sugar, ½ cup flour** and **½ cup vinegar.** Cook and remove from heat. Add **1 tablespoon butter.** Cool. Add **1 cup mayonnaise** and **⅛ cup mustard.** Chill overnight.

### Bean Salad

⅔ cup vinegar  
⅓ cup salad oil  
1 green pepper, chopped  
1 can yellow wax beans  
1 cup sugar  
1 onion, chopped  
1 can green beans  
1 can kidney beans

Combine all ingredients. Let set overnight in refrigerator before serving.

**Notes:**

# Crab and Chicken

### Crab Meat Salad

½ lb. shrimp
Onions, chopped fine
Mayonnaise
1 lb. crabmeat

Celery, chopped fine
Cavender®'s Greek seasoning to taste

Mix all ingredients and chill.

### Hot Chicken Salad

2 cups diced, cooked chicken
½ cup slivered almonds, toasted
1 tablespoon chopped onion
1½ teaspoons grated lemon rind
½ teaspoon pepper
1½ cups crushed potato chips

1½ cups diced celery
2 hard-cooked eggs, chopped
1 cup mayonnaise
2 teaspoons lemon juice
1½ cups (6 oz) shredded Cheddar cheese

Combine chicken, celery, almonds, eggs, onion, mayonnaise, lemon rind, lemon juice, and pepper in a large bowl. Mix well. Spoon chicken mixture into a lightly greased shallow 2 qt. casserole. Sprinkle with cheese and top with potato chips. Bake at 375 degrees for 25 minutes. Yield: 6 servings.

Notes:

# Salads

### Tropical Chicken Salad

| | |
|---|---|
| 4 chicken breasts, cooked, deboned | 1½ cups small, seedless white grapes |
| 1 tablespoon salad oil | 1 cup chopped celery |
| 2 tablespoons orange juice | 1 cup pineapple tidbits, drained |
| 1 tablespoon vinegar | 1 (11 oz) can mandarin oranges, drained |
| ½ teaspoon salt | |
| 1 cup mayonnaise | ½ cup slivered almonds or pecans |

Combine chicken, oil, orange juice, vinegar and salt. Refrigerate chicken while assembling remaining ingredients. Right before serving, gently toss all ingredients. Serve on a bed of lettuce or serve in fresh pineapple halves.

# Molded Salads

### Flossie's Cranberry Casserole

| | |
|---|---|
| 3 cups diced, unpeeled apples | 1 cup sugar |
| 2 cups raw cranberries | ½ cup water |

Put apples and cranberries into 9" square Pyrex® dish. Sprinkle with sugar. Pour water on top.

Topping:

| | |
|---|---|
| 1 stick melted butter | ½ cup flour |
| 1½ cups instant oatmeal | ½ cup chopped pecans |
| ½ cup packed brown sugar | |

Mix ingredients. Sprinkle over cranberries and apples. Bake 1 hour at 350°.

Notes:

### 7-Up® Salad

2 (3 oz) pkgs. strawberry-banana gelatin
2 (7 oz) bottles of 7-Up®
1 (#303) can crushed pineapple
1 egg
1 tablespoon margarine or butter
1 contained Cool Whip®
Chopped pecans
3 cups boiling water
3 bananas, sliced
½ cup sugar
2 tablespoons flour
1 cup pineapple juice
1 (3 oz) pkg. cream cheese

Dissolve gelatin in boiling water. Allow to cool slightly and stir in 7-Up®. Let chill until almost syrupy.

Drain pineapple and reserve juice, add pineapple and bananas to gelatin mixture. Pour into 9x13-inch pan. Chill until firm.

For *Topping*, add water to pineapple juice to make 1 cup. In sauce pan, blend sugar, flour, juice and egg, stirring over low heat until thickened. Cool. Add butter and cook. Whip softened cream cheese and add to sauce mixture. Spread over congealed salad. Use Cool Whip® and chopped pecans, if desired.

*"Another good thing about telling the truth is that you don't have to remember what you said."*

Notes:

# Salads

## Congealed Salad

1 small pkg. peach Jello®  
1 small can crushed pineapple in heavy syrup  
3 tablespoons sugar

Mix together. Put on stove and bring to boil. Set aside to cool.

Add:

1 (8 oz) Cool Whip®  
2 cups buttermilk  
1½ cups chopped pecans

Stir and mix well. Pour into a mold and let set overnight. (Grease mold with corn oil).

## Congealed Fruit Salad

2 pkgs. Jello® (Lemon or Lime)  
1 cup pineapple juice (heated to dissolve Jello®)  
1 cup fresh orange juice  
⅔ cup pineapple chunks  
⅔ cup fresh orange sections  
½ cup nuts  
½ pint whipping cream, whipped

Mix Jello® and heated pineapple juice. Chill. Beat together. Blend in whipped cream. Add orange sections, pineapple chunks and nuts. Blend together and place in mold. Chill until firm.

Notes:

### Betty's Cranberry Salad

1 lb. cranberries
2 cups sugar
2 oranges, seeds removed
2 apples
1 pkg. raspberry Jello®
1 pkg. orange Jello®
1¼ cups boiling water
½ to 1 cup chopped nuts

Dissolve Jello® and sugar in boiling water. Chill until slightly thickened. Add ground fruits and nuts.

### Holiday Cranberry Salad

1 pkg. cranberries
1 cup sugar
1 pt. whipping cream
1 cup chopped nuts (pecans)
1 pkg. miniature marshmallows
1 small can crushed pineapples, drained

Grind cranberries and add sugar. Let set 1 hour. Add whipped cream and marshmallows. Let set 1 hour. Add pineapple and nuts. Set overnight.

### Perfection Salad

1 envelope unflavored gelatin
¼ cup cold water
1 cup hot water
¼ cup sugar
½ teaspoon salt
¼ cup vinegar
1 tablespoon lemon juice
½ cup finely chopped cabbage
1 cup chopped celery
2 tablespoons chopped pimento

Soften gelatin in cold water. Dissolve in hot water. Add sugar and salt. Stir until dissolved. Add vinegar and lemon juice. Cool. When mixture begins to thicken, add remaining ingredients. Turn into molds.

**Notes:**

*Salads* 43

## Pineapple and Strawberry Molds

1 can crushed pineapples
1 pkg. lime Jello®
¼ cup lemon juice
1 (8 oz) pkg. cream cheese

1 (16 oz) pkg. frozen strawberries
1 pkg. strawberry Jello®
½ cup chopped nuts

Drain pineapple. Add water to pineapple juice to make 1½ cups. Heat to boiling and use to dissolve Jello®. Cool. Add lemon juice. Beat softened cream cheese with egg beater until light and fluffy, and then beat into Jello® mixture. Add crushed pineapple and fill 10 individual molds half full.

Thaw strawberries and drain off juice. Add water to juice to make 1½ cups. Heat to boiling and use to dissolve Jello®. Chill until syrupy and then beat with egg beater until light and fluffy. Fold in strawberries and nuts and fill molds. Chill until firm.

## Pretzel Salad

2⅔ cups pretzels, broken up
8 oz. cream cheese
2 cups Cool Whip®
1 large can crushed pineapple

1½ sticks margarine, melted
1 cup sugar
10 oz. strawberries
1 pkg. strawberry Jello®

Mix pretzels and margarine. Spread in bottom of dish. Combine cream cheese, sugar and Cool Whip®. Spread over pretzels. Refrigerate until set.

Drain strawberries and pineapple. Add water to juices to make 2 cups. Heat with strawberry Jello®. Add fruit. Spread over salad. Refrigerate.

Notes:

## Sparkling Fruit Mold

1 (16 oz) can peach slices
1 (8¼ oz) can pineapple chunks
2 (3 oz) pkgs. orange gelatin
1¼ cups boiling water
¾ cup sparkling rosé wine or ginger ale
1 cup miniature marshmallows
1 cup heavy cream, whipped
½ cup Miracle Whip® Salad Dressing

Drain fruit; reserve syrup. Dissolve gelatin in boiling water. Add wine. Add cold water to syrup to make 1¾ cups; stir into gelatin. Chill until partially set; fold in fruit. Pour into 2-quart bowl; chill until firm. Fold marshmallows and whipped cream into salad dressing. Spoon over gelatin; chill. Garnish with toasted shredded coconut, if desired. 10 servings.

## Strawberry-Pretzel Salad

*First Layer:* Mix together **2 cups crushed, thin pretzels,** ¾ **cup melted margarine and 3 tablespoons sugar.** Pat into 9x13″ pan. Bake at 400° for 6 minutes.

*Second Layer:* Mix together **1 (8 oz) pkg. softened cream cheese, 2 cups whipped topping and** ¾ **cup sugar.** Spread over baked, cooled crust. Chill.

*Third Layer:* Mix **1 (6 oz) pkg. strawberry Jello® dissolved in 2 cups boiling water, 2 (10 oz) pkgs. of frozen strawberries, not drained.** Cool and put on top of other two layers.

*"It's not money that makes you rich."*

Notes:

# Fruit Salads

### Blueberry Salad

1 cup pecans
2 small pkgs. strawberry Jello®
2 cups hot water
Pecans

1 can blueberries (reserve juice)
1 can (13 oz) crushed pineapple, (reserve juice)

Dissolve Jello® in hot water. Add can of blueberries and pineapples with natural juices. Add pecans. Congeal overnight.

Beat together 1 (8 oz) pkg. cream cheese and ½ cup sour cream. Add ½ cup sugar. Make this topping just before serving. Garnish with pecans.

### Cherry-Orange Salad

¼ cup frozen orange juice concentrate, thawed
½ cup whipping cream, whipped
1 (11 oz) can mandarin oranges, drained
2 cups green grapes

2 eggs, beaten
¼ cup sugar
2 (17 oz) jars light or dark sweet cherries, drained and pitted
2 cups miniature marshmallows

Combine orange juice, eggs, and sugar in a small saucepan. Cook over low heat, stirring constantly until thickened. Cool. Fold whipped cream into orange juice mixture. Add remaining ingredients, stirring gently until coated. Chill. Yield: 8 to 10 servings.

Notes:

### Frozen Fruit Salad

2 (3 oz) pkgs. cream cheese
1 cup mayonnaise
1 cup heavy cream, whipped
2½ cups crushed, drained pineapples
½ cup red maraschino cherries, quartered
½ cup green maraschino cherries, quartered
2½ cups miniature marshmallows

Combine cream cheese and mayonnaise. Blend until smooth. Fold in whipped cream, fruit and marshmallows. Pour into 1 quart refrigerator tray. Freeze until firm. Serve on crisp lettuce.

### Flossie's Fruit Salad

1 cup shredded coconut
1 cup sour cream
1 cup mandarin oranges
1 cup miniature Kraft® marshmallows
1 cup pineapples
1 cup maraschino cherries

Drain juices from canned fruits. Mix together and chill. Garnish with maraschino cherries.

### Betty's Fruit Salad

1 large ctn. cottage cheese
1 large can pineapple chunks, drained
1 small can coconut, if desired
1 large Cool Whip®
1 can mandarin oranges, drained
1 (3 oz) pkg. orange Jello,® dry

Mix cottage cheese, Cool Whip,® and Jello.® Add other ingredients. Mix well and refrigerate.

**Notes:**

### Glazed Fruit

1 can Mandarin oranges
1 can sliced peaches
Maraschino cherries
Melon — honeydew and
 cantaloupe, when in season

1 can chunk pineapple
2 red apples, diced
Bananas
White seedless grapes
Strawberries

Sauce:

1 cup juice from fruit
1 (3 oz) pkg. vanilla pudding

¼ cup Tang®

Cook sauce until it boils. Cool. Prepare fruit, except bananas. Pour sauce over fruit. Add bananas last and toss lightly.

# Salad Dressing

### Salad Dressing

1 cup sugar
6 teaspoons Salad Delight® or Salad
 Seasoning

2 (8 oz) bottles Creamy Italian Dressing
6 teaspoons vinegar
Dash of garlic salt

Mix together and shake well.

Notes:

# Vegetables

*"A Friend is the first person who comes in, when the whole world has gone out"*

# *Vegetables*

# Asparagus

### Asparagus Casserole

1 large can Green Giant,® asparagus
1 can mushroom soup, undiluted
5 or 6 slices American Cheese, grated

Cracker crumbs
Pimento
Butter
Slivered almonds

Drain juices from asparagus, saving juice. Place asparagus in casserole. Add soup and cheese. Add a good coverage layer of cracker crumbs. Dot with butter. Can use some strips of pimento to give color if desired. Almonds are good on top (optional). Bake at 325° for 20 to 25 minutes, until it bubbles up. This recipe can be doubled for a large group and it works well.

### Asparagus-Water Chestnut Casserole

2 cans asparagus, drained
2 cans Cheddar cheese soup
Buttered bread crumbs

1 (5 oz) can Chun King® water chestnuts, sliced

Place asparagus, water chestnuts, and soup in alternate layers in a 2-qt. greased casserole dish. Top with buttered bread crumbs. Heat until bubbly hot in 350° oven. Serves 8-10.

**Notes:**

# Broccoli

### Broccoli Bake

2 boxes frozen chopped broccoli
1 cup sharp cheese, grated
Salt and pepper to taste
2 eggs, well beaten
½ pkg. Pepperidge Farm® stuffing

1 cup mayonnaise
½ stick margarine
1 can mushroom soup
1 med. onion, chopped

Drain cooked broccoli, combining soup, mayonnaise, eggs, onion, salt and pepper. Pour in 8x8" pan. Sprinkle cheese on top. Melt margarine and add to stuffing and pour on top. Bake at 350° for 45 minutes.

### Broccoli Bread

1 box Jiffy® cornbread mix
4 eggs, beaten
1 stick margarine, melted
1 small onion, chopped

1 pkg. frozen chopped broccoli, thawed
6 oz. cottage cheese
Dash of salt

Melt butter, add all other ingredients except Jiffy.® Mix well. Add Jiffy.® Put in greased 9 x 13 pan. Bake at 350° for 15 minutes.

Notes:

# Vegetables

### Kath's Broccoli Casserole

4 boxes (10 oz) frozen broccoli
1 cup mayonnaise
¼ stick margarine
1 can cream of mushroom soup
½ cup Italian bread crumbs
1 cup sharp grated cheese

Cook broccoli as directed on pkg. Drain and add margarine. In bowl, add mayonnaise and soup together. Mix well. Add bread crumbs and broccoli to soup mixture. Stir well. Pour into large glass baking dish. Sprinkle with cheese. Bake 35 minutes at 350°. Remove from oven to wire rack until ready to serve.

### Broccoli Casserole of North Carolina

2 pkgs. chopped, cooked and drained broccoli
1 can mushroom soup
½ cup margarine
2 eggs, well-beaten
1 cup sharp grated cheese
1 med. onion, chopped fine
½ pkg. Pepperidge Farm® corn bread dressing
salt and pepper to taste

Add margarine, onion and cheese to hot broccoli. Let cool and then add mushroom soup, beaten eggs, salt, and pepper. Mix well. Bake in casserole 20 minutes at 350°. Remove from oven and top with half pkg. Pepperidge Farm® corn bread dressing. Dot with margarine. Bake 10 minutes.

Notes:

## Betty Jane's Broccoli Casserole

2 pkgs. frozen broccoli, chopped or spears
1 cup grated cheddar cheese, medium sharp
¼ cup slivered almonds or pecans
1 can cream of mushroom soup, undiluted
1 stick butter or margarine
½ cup seasoned croutons

Cook broccoli according to package directions. Heat soup and cheese together until heated through and cheese is melted. Place broccoli in casserole, and pour soup/cheese mixture over it. Sprinkle with seasoned croutons. Pour melted butter or margarine over the top. Sprinkle nuts on top. Heat in 350° oven until croutons are golden brown and casserole is heated through.

## Ardette's Broccoli Casserole

2 (10 oz) pkgs. frozen broccoli spears
1 cup mayonnaise
1 roll of Ritz® crackers, crushed
1 can cream of chicken soup
3 eggs
1 cup grated sharp cheese
½ stick margarine, melted

Cut broccoli into chunks while still frozen. Thaw in microwave on high power level for 4 minutes. Drain. Mix chicken soup, eggs and mayonnaise real good then add cheese. Add this mixture to broccoli and toss together. Pour into greased 8x11 inch baking dish. Crush crackers and add margarine. Cover top of casserole with crackers and bake 30 minutes in 350° oven.

Notes:

# Vegetables

## Broccoli and Chicken

2 pkgs. frozen broccoli spears, cooked and drained

3½ cups precooked chicken

Place broccoli in dish. Place chicken on top of broccoli. Make a White Sauce.

*White Sauce*

½ stick margarine
1½ cups milk

2½ tablespoons flour
1 cup shredded cheddar cheese

Bring to a boil. Add 1 cup of shredded cheese. Cook until melted. Pour over chicken. Bake at 300° until hot. Serves 6.

## Broccoli Cornbread

1 box chopped broccoli
1 large onion, chopped
1 stick margarine, melted
4 eggs, well beaten

1 box Jiffy® cornbread mix
6 oz. cottage cheese
1 teaspoon salt

Add all ingredients together with the cornbread mix being last. Pour into greased 9x13-inch pan and bake at 400° for 30 minutes or until done.

Notes:

### Broccoli and Rice Casserole

2 (10 oz) pkg. broccoli, cooked
½ cup chopped onion
1 can cream of mushroom soup
2 cups Minute Rice®, cooked
½ cup chopped celery
1 small jar Cheeze Whiz®

Cook broccoli, onion and celery together. Cook rice. Mix all ingredients together and pour in baking dish. Bake at 350° for 20 minutes.

### Broccoli Soup

2 pkg. chopped frozen broccoli
2 or 3 med. potatoes
1 bay leaf
Butter
1 med. onion, chopped
Milk
Chicken broth

Cook broccoli, onions, potatoes and bay leaf until broccoli is tender. Remove bay leaf. Put the rest in blender and puree. Pour into sauce pan. Add chicken broth, butter and milk. Bring almost to a boil. Add salt and pepper to taste. *(I stew a chicken and use broth).*

*"In my garden, Love grows"*

Notes:

# Cabbage

### Cabbage Casserole

1 head cabbage, chopped
1 med. onion, chopped
½ green pepper, chopped
½ cup milk
5 slices white bread, cubed
salt and pepper to taste

8 slices bacon, fried until crisp
    and chopped
2 cans cream of chicken soup
8 oz. cheddar cheese, grated
1 stick butter, melted

Cook cabbage in salted water 8 minutes and drain. Sauté onions and green pepper in bacon drippings. Mix cabbage, bacon, onions, green peppers, soup, milk, cheese and turn into casseroles. Top with buttered bread crumbs. Bake at 350° for 20-30 minutes or until bubbly.

### Cabbage Rolls

1 lb. ground beef
1 lb. pork sausage
½ cup rice (dry, uncooked)
1 small onion, chopped

12 wilted cabbage leaves
Black pepper
1 qt. tomatoes

Mix meat, salt, pepper, rice, and onion together. Wilt cabbage leaves in boiling water. Roll small amount of meat mixture into a ball. Roll into cabbage leaf and fasten end with a toothpick. Place cabbage rolls in cooker and cover with 1 quart tomatoes. Simmer for 2 hours.

**Notes:**

## Chow Chow

1 gallon chopped cabbage
½ gallon chopped green tomatoes
2 cups sugar
3½ cups vinegar

1 quart chopped onion
6 chopped green peppers
Red peppers (optional)

Soak all vegetables in salt water overnight except onions. Drain well next morning. Add the onions, sugar, vinegar, and some red peppers if you like it hot. Mix well and cook 30 minutes. Seal in pint jars.

# Carrots

## Copper Pennies

2 lbs. fresh carrots, sliced ¼-inch rounds
2 med. onions, thinly sliced and separated in rings
1 med. green pepper, cut in strips
1 (10-¾ oz) can tomato soup, undiluted

¾ cup vinegar
½ cup cooking oil
1 teaspoon prepared mustard
⅔ cup sugar
1 teaspoon Worcestershire® sauce
½ teaspoon salt

Cook carrots 8-10 minutes in small amount of water. Drain and combine with all other ingredients. Mix well. Cover and marinate in refrigerator overnight. Can be served hot or cold.

Notes:

# Corn

### Corn Souffle

1 (16 oz) can creamed corn
1 stick melted margarine
2 eggs

1 (16 oz) can kernel corn
1 (8 oz) carton sour cream
1 box Jiffy® cornmeal mix

Mix together all ingredients and put into a 2-qt casserole dish and bake at 350° for 45 minutes, until golden brown.

# Mushrooms

### Mushrooms

4 lbs. fresh mushrooms
1 qt. burgundy wine
4 beef bouillon cubes
1 tablespoon accent
2 tablespoons Worcestershire® sauce

1 lb. butter
4 chicken bouillon cubes
2 cups water
1 tablespoon garlic powder

Mix all ingredients. Simmer 4 hours covered. Simmer 4 hours uncovered.

### Mushroom Roast

1 3-4 lb. beef roast
1 can cream of mushroom soup
1 can cream of onion soup

3 cans water
salt and pepper to taste
1 tablespoon flour

Shake flour in an oven cooking bag. Place roast in bag. Add remaining ingredients. Bake 2½ to 3 hours at 350° or until done.

## Stuffed Mushrooms

1 lb. large, fresh mushrooms
1 med. onion, chopped fine
1 stick butter
salt and pepper to taste

1 pkg. Pepperidge® stuffing
3 stalks celery, chopped fine
1 can chicken broth
Poultry seasoning

Wash mushrooms and remove stems. Chop stems, onions, and celery, and sauté in butter until soft. Mix stuffing mix, sautéed vegetables, broth and season to taste. Stuff mushrooms with stuffing mixture. Bake at 350° for 30 minutes or until beginning to brown on top and mushrooms are tender. Serve hot.

# Onions

## Betty Jane's Onion Soup

4 cans beef bouillon
1 stick butter
Dash of Kitchen Bouquet®
Sherry to taste (¼ cup start)
½ large can Parmesan cheese, grated

4 or 5 cans of water
5 med. onions (halved, then slice)
2 tablespoons sugar
Grated Black Diamond® Cheese or Canadian Cheddar
Toasted French Bread, thinly sliced

Sauté onions in butter until tender. Add dash of Kitchen Bouquet.® Add beef bouillon and water. Add sugar and ½ can of Parmesan cheese. Simmer 1 hour. Add sherry. Put grated Black Diamond® in bottom of crock (just enough to cover bottom). Pour hot soup over that and add toasted French Bread in slices. Top with more grated Black Diamond® cheese. Bake in 500° oven until cheese melts and is bubbly, almost brown.

Notes:

# Vegetables

## Marinated Cucumbers and Onions

1 cup water
¼ cup vinegar
4 medium cucumbers
4 medium onions
¼ cup sugar
Parsley & chives for garnish
2 dashes of garlic salt

Mix water, vinegar, sugar and salt. Cut cucumbers and onions and stir into mixture. Sprinkle parsley and chives on top. Chill for 4 hours.

# Potatoes

## Fried Potato Cake

1 dish of left-over mashed potatoes
2 tablespoons flour
1 small onion, chopped fine
Salt and pepper to taste

Pat out potato cakes and fry in hot oil or bacon fat until golden brown on both sides.

## Grated Sweet Potato Yams

4 cups grated peeled sweet potatoes
1 cup sugar
Cinnamon
Marshmallows
Salted ice water
1 cup undiluted evaporated milk
½ cup milk
⅔ stick margarine

Soak potatoes in salted ice water for 15 minutes, drain thoroughly and combine with sugar, evaporated milk and whole milk. Turn into buttered baking dish. Sprinkle with cinnamon. Dot with margarine. Bake in 350° oven for a little over an hour or until potatoes are done. Remove from oven. Top with miniature marshmallows. Place back in oven to melt marshmallows.

### Portuguese Potato Casserole

8-10 potatoes, cubed and cooked
1 lb. Velveeta® cheese, cubed
⅓ onion, chopped
1 small jar pimentos, chopped
3 slices of bread, cubed

2 tablespoons parsley
1 teaspoon paprika
1 teaspoon garlic
2 sticks margarine, melted

Place potatoes in baking dish. Add onions and half of cheese. Cover with bread cubes. Sprinkle with pimento, parsley, paprika and garlic. Add remaining cheese. Pour margarine over entire dish. Bake at 350° for approximately 30-45 minutes.

### Potato Casserole

2 (1 lb) bags frozen hash brown potatoes
1 (8 oz) ctn. sour cream
1 (8 oz) cheese, grated

Salt and pepper to taste
½ onion, diced
1 can Cream of Chicken soup
⅔ stick margarine, melted

Thaw potatoes until crumbly. Mix with salt and pepper to taste. Mix with other ingredients. Bake at 375° for 60 minutes.

**Notes:**

*Vegetables*

## Shredded Yams

2 lb. raw sweet potatoes
1 tablespoon salt
½ cup white corn syrup
1 cup pineapple juice

1 gal. water
1 cup sugar
½ cup water
4 tablespoons butter or margarine

Shred yams into a gallon of water with salt added. Combine sugar, syrup, and water in a heavy saucepan and cook until it forms a light syrup. Drain potatoes, rinse and pat dry. Place in a heat resistant 12x6x3-inch glass baking dish. Pour pineapple juice over potatoes, then pour the cooked syrup over potatoes. Dot with butter. Bake uncovered at 350° about 35 minutes or until done. Yield: 12 servings.

## Gladys' Sweet Potatoes Casserole

4 medium sweet potatoes
Nutmeg
1¼ cups water

1½ sticks butter
1¾ cups sugar

*Pastry:* **2 cups flour, 1 teaspoon salt, 1 cup shortening, and a little water.**

Cut shortening into flour and salt. Add water to make dough. Roll thinly. Put sliced potatoes in bottom of casserole. Add dash of nutmeg and ½ cup sugar. Dot with butter. Cover with strips of pastry. Repeat layer and top with remaining sugar, nutmeg, and butter. Pour water over this. Cover with pastry. Bake at 375°-400° for about 1 hour or until crust is crisp and potatoes are done.

Notes:

### Autumn Sweet Potato Casserole

3 cups sweet potatoes, cooked
⅓ stick margarine
1 cup sugar
½ cup milk
1 teaspoon sherry flavoring
1 teaspoon butter flavoring
2 eggs

Mix above ingredients in blender. Pour into baking dish.

Mix 1/3 stick margarine, 1 cup brown sugar, and 1 cup chopped pecans. Pour over mixture in baking dish. Bake for 35 minutes at 350°.

### Sweet Potato Casserole with Crunchy Topping

3 cups mashed potatoes
½ teaspoon salt
⅓ cup Eagle Brand® Sweetened Condensed Milk
⅓ cup sugar (or more)
⅓ stick margarine, melted
1 teaspoon butter flavoring
2 eggs, beaten

Combine potatoes, sugar, salt, margarine, milk, flavoring and eggs; turn into greased baking dish.

Sprinkle with topping made by blending:

1 cup brown sugar
⅓ stick margarine
⅓ cup flour
1 cup chopped walnuts

Bake in oven at 350° for 35 minutes.

**Notes:**

# Vegetables

### Sweet Potato Souffle

3 cups cooked mashed potatoes  
1 cup sugar  
2 eggs  
½ cup milk  
½ teaspoon salt  
1 teaspoon vanilla  
½ teaspoon pumpkin pie spices  

Mix all ingredients and pour into buttered pan.

1 cup brown sugar  
½ cup flour  
1 cup chopped pecans  
½ stick butter  

Combine above ingredients and spread over potato mixture. Bake at 400° for 30-40 minutes or until brown on top.

# Spinach

### Creamy Spinach Casserole

2 (10 oz) pkgs. frozen spinach, chopped  
½ cup chopped onion  
¼ cup seasoned bread crumbs  
1 (8 oz) pkg. cream cheese  
¼ cup melted butter  

Cook spinach in small amount of water until thawed. Drain in colander. Squeeze dry. While still warm, combine with cream cheese and 2 tablespoons butter, until cheese is melted. Stir in chopped onion. Spoon into greased baking dish. Top with bread crumbs. Drizzle with remaining butter. Bake, uncovered at 350° for 20 minutes.

Notes:

# Squash

### Lo's Mixture

6 cups yellow squash, sliced
½ cup onion, chopped
½ teaspoon salt
1 stick butter

1 pkg. Pepperidge Farm® dressing
1 can cream of chicken soup
1 (8 oz) sour cream
1 cup grated carrots

Preheat oven to 350°. Butter a large casserole dish. Cook squash and onions in a small amount of salted water until tender. Combine melted margarine and stuffing mix. Drain squash and onion; add soup and sour cream; fold in carrots.

Pour squash mixture into casserole dish and top with dressing. Bake at 350° for 25 to 30 minutes.

*"There are many tears in the heart, that never reach the eye"*

Notes:

# Vegetables

### Grandma's Squash Casserole

1 egg, beaten
½ onion, chopped
1 can cream of chicken soup
½ cup margarine
1½ cups bread crumbs
1 stick margarine, melted
½ cup cracker crumbs
2½ cups cooked squash, mashed

Combine all ingredients except crumb mixture and margarine in a greased pan. Combine crumb mixture and melted margarine and put on top. Cook at 275° for 40 minutes or until brown.

### Squash Casserole

2 lbs. squash, cooked in salted water, cook
1 raw carrot finely chopped
1 onion finely chopped
1 tablespoon pimento finely chopped
1 can cream of chicken soup
½ pt. sour cream
1½ cups herb stuffing
1 stick butter

Mix first six ingredients. Melt butter. Add to stuffing mix. Add only half of this to squash. Sprinkle the rest on top. Bake 30 minutes at 350°. Cover. Bake 20-25 minutes longer.

### Yellow Squash Casserole

2 med. squash, sliced thin
1 can cream of chicken soup
1 small onion, chopped
1 small pkg. shredded Cheddar cheese
1 cup bread crumbs

Boil squash and onion in shallow pan for 10 minutes or until tender. Drain. Mix with undiluted soup and place in casserole dish. Cover with cheese and then bread crumbs. Bake at 425° for 30 minutes or until bubbly.

Notes:

# Tomatoes

### Marinated Tomatoes

1/3 cup vegetable oil
2 tablespoons onion, thinly sliced
1/2 teaspoon salt
1/8 teaspoon pepper
2 tablespoons wine vinegar

2 tablespoons fresh parsley, chopped
1/4 teaspoon dried whole marjoram
3 med. tomatoes, peeled and
 quartered

**Combine first 7 ingredients** in a jar. Cover tightly and shake vigorously. Pour over tomatoes, cover and marinate 6 to 8 hours. 4-6 servings.

# Vegetable Casseroles

### Claudine's Vegetable Casserole

1 cup chopped onions
1 cup chopped celery
1 (1 lb., 1 oz) can green peas
1 (4 oz) jar pimentos, drained
 and chopped

1 cup chopped bell peppers
1 stick margarine
1 can mushroom soup
bread crumbs

Sauté onions, pepper and celery in melted margarine until tender but not brown. Put drained peas and pimento in a greased oblong casserole dish. Add cooked vegetables and mushroom soup. Mix all together and sprinkle top with bread crumbs. Bake 20 minutes in 350° oven. Serves 6-8.

**Notes:**

### Flossie's Vegetable Casserole

1 (16 oz) can shoe peg corn
1 cup chopped green pepper
1 (16 oz) can French-style green beans
1 (10-1/4 oz) can cream of celery
4 cups cheese crackers
1 cup chopped celery
1 cup chopped onion
1 cup sour cream
1 cup grated Cheddar cheese
2 oz slivered almonds
1/2 cup melted butter

Drain canned vegetables and combine with celery, onion, green pepper, cheese, sour cream and soup. Place mixture in a 9x13-inch baking pan. Crumble crackers with almonds and melted butter. Sprinkle on top of casserole mixture. Bake for 30 to 45 minutes or until bubbly in a 350° oven.

### Vegetable Casserole
*(This is delightful!)*

2 cans Veg-All® vegetables, drained
1 cup chopped onion
1 cup mayonnaise
1 cup chopped celery
1 can water chestnuts, sliced and drained
1 cup grated cheddar cheese
Cheese crackers

Mix all ingredients except crackers. Spread in long casserole dish and top with crushed cheese crackers which have been mixed with margarine, or top with cheese crackers, plain. Bake 30 minutes at 350°.

Notes:

### Veg-All® Casserole

2 (16 oz) cans Veg-All®  
1 cup chopped celery  
1 (10-¾ oz) can cream of chicken soup  
1 (8 oz) can water chestnuts  
1 cup chopped onions  
¾ cup mayonnaise

*Topping:* **1 stick margarine, melted** and mixed with **1 stack Ritz® crackers.**

Drain Veg-All® and chestnuts. Mix with remaining ingredients. Pour into 2-quart or two 1 quart baking dishes. Bake 30 minutes at 350°. After baking, pour on topping. Bake an additional 10 minutes longer.

*"God gives the best to those who leave the choice to Him"*

Notes:

# Punch

*"Enrich someone's life today with a warm word of praise.
Both of you will be better for it"*

### Amy Gormby's Punch

46 oz. Orange Hawaiian Punch®  
1 lemon sliced  
12 inches of cinnamon sticks  
2 oranges sliced, for garnish  

46 oz. apricot nectar  
6 whole allspice  
4 cloves  

Mix. Serve warm.

### Christmas Eve Punch

1 (32 oz) bottle cranberry juice cocktail  
1 (46 oz) can unsweetened pineapple juice  
2 cups orange juice  

½ cup sugar  
1 (33.8 oz) bottle ginger ale, chilled  
⅔ cup lemon juice  
2 teaspoons almond extract  

Combine cranberry juice, pineapple juice, orange juice, sugar, lemon juice, and almond extract. To serve, add ginger ale, stirring well.

### Creamy Strawberry Punch

1 (10 oz) pkg. frozen strawberries, thawed  
½ gal. pineapple sherbet, softened  

1 (28 oz) bottle ginger ale  
Fresh strawberries, optional  

Place strawberries in container of an electric blender. Process until pureed. Pour into punch bowl. Add ginger ale and sherbet. Stir until creamy. Serve immediately. Garnish with fresh strawberries, if desired.

**Notes:**

### Fruit Punch

2 pkgs. Jello® (cherry or lime)
2 cups sugar (more if needed)
2 qts. pineapple juice

2 cans frozen orange juice, diluted
2 qts. ginger ale

Dissolve Jello® and sugar in about a quart of hot water. Cool and add juices and more sugar, if desired. Add ice cubes and ginger ale before serving.

### Hot Cran-Apple Cider

4 qts. apple cider
½ cup brown sugar, packed
3 teaspoons cloves

3 qts. cranberry cocktail
8 sticks cinnamon
1 teaspoon nutmeg

Heat and simmer 15-20 minutes. Serve with 1 package **red hots.** Makes 50 servings.

### Paradise Island Punch

1 cup water
1 cup sugar
1 qt. pineapple juice
Juice of 2 oranges
Juice of lemon
Juice of ½ grapefruit

½ cup crushed pineapple
⅓ cup crushed strawberries
2 qts. cranberry juice
1 qt. apple juice
1 qt. ginger ale

Dissolve 1 cup sugar in 1 cup hot water. Add all other ingredients and mix. Do not add ginger ale until ready to serve. Serves 50.

**Notes:**

## Wassail Bowl

3 oranges  
Whole cloves  
2 qts. apple cider or juice  

½ cup lemon juice  
½ cup sugar  
Cinnamon sticks  

Set oven at 350°. Push cloves, about ¼ inch apart, into oranges. Place in a shallow pan. Bake 30 minutes. Heat apple cider or juice, sugar and several cinnamon sticks, until small bubbles appear around edge. Remove from heat and stir in lemon juice. Pour into heatproof punch bowl. With ice pick, pierce oranges in several places. Add to cider. Serve in mugs and use cinnamon sticks to stir if desired.

**Notes:**

# Breads, Pasta and Rice

*"A house is not a home, unless it provides food and warmth for the soul as well as for the body"*

## Baked Cheese Grits

4 cups water
1 cup uncooked regular grits
½ cup butter or margarine
1 teaspoon Worcestershire® sauce
Fresh mushroom slices

1 teaspoon salt
1 cup (4 oz) shredded sharp cheddar cheese
3 eggs, slightly beaten
Fresh parsley sprigs

Bring water and salt to a boil. Stir in grits. Cook grits about 30 minutes or until done. Remove from heat and add cheese, margarine, and Worcestershire® sauce. Stir until cheese and butter melt.

Gradually stir about ¼ of hot grits into eggs. Add remaining grits, stirring well. Pour grits into lightly greased 9" quiche dish. Bake at 350° for one hour. Garnish with mushrooms and parsley.

## Christmas Rice

1 cup raw rice
2 cans chicken soup with rice
1¼ cups water
1 stick margarine

1 bell pepper, sliced
1 small jar pimento
1 can mushrooms (optional)
1 medium onion, chopped

Mix all ingredients in 2-quart casserole dish. Bake for 45 minutes to 1 hour in a 350° oven. Stir twice while cooking.

Notes:

## Fast Rolls

1 cup hot water (105°-115°)
1 cup Crisco® oil
1 to 1¼ cups sugar
2 eggs, beaten
4 cups white unsifted flour

2 pkgs. yeast (dissolved in hot water)
1½ teaspoons salt
1 cup cold water
2 cups wheat unsifted flour

Mix until blended. *(I let it rise for a few hours, but it can be baked immediately).* Bake in greased muffin tins *(I also let it rise again in tins)* at 400° until light brown (12 to 15 minutes). Dough will keep 1 week in refrigerator.

## Good Morning Muffins

1¼ cups sugar
2¼ cups flour
3 teaspoons cinnamon
2 teaspoons baking soda
½ teaspoon salt
½ cup coconut
½ cup raisins

2 cups grated carrots
1 large grated apple
8 oz. crushed pineapple, drained
½ cup chopped pecans
3 eggs
1 cup vegetable oil
1 teaspoon vanilla

Sift together sugar, flour, cinnamon, baking soda, and salt into mixing bowl. Add the fruit, carrots and nuts. Stir to combine. Beat the eggs, oil, and vanilla together. Pour this mixture in the bowl with dry ingredients. Blend well. Spoon batter into lined cupcake tins. Fill each cup to the brim. Bake in 350° oven for 35 minutes or until done. Cool muffins in pan for 10 minutes. Turn out to finish cooking on rack.

**Notes:**

## Hilda's Corn Souffle

1 (16 oz) can creamed corn
1 (16 oz) can kernel corn
1 stick margarine (melted)
1 (8 oz) carton sour cream
2 eggs
1 box Jiffy® cornmeal mix

Mix all ingredients. Put in a 2 quart casserole dish. Bake at 350° for 45 minutes until golden brown.

## Monkey Bread

2 cans refrigerated buttermilk biscuits
½ cup pecan or walnut pieces
¾ cup butter
¾ cup brown sugar (packed)
¼ cup white sugar

*Cinnamon-sugar mixture:*

4 tablespoons sugar
2-3 teaspoons cinnamon (to taste)

Cut each biscuit into 4 pieces. Press a piece of pecan or walnut into each. Put cinnamon mixture into a bag and shake each biscuit piece in mixture. Place into a greased bundt or angel food pan. Bring butter and sugars to a rolling boil and pour over biscuits. Bake 30 minutes at 350°. Remove from pan immediately. Leave in ring to serve.

**Notes:**

### Flossie's Zucchini Bread

3 eggs
2 cups sugar
1 cup oil
2 cups zucchini, peeled, grated
3 cups flour
1 teaspoon baking soda

1 teaspoon baking powder
1 teaspoon salt
3 teaspoons cinnamon
2 teaspoons vanilla
½ cup chopped nuts

Beat eggs until light and foamy. Add sugar, oil, zucchini and vanilla and set aside mixture. In separate bowl, sift flour, soda, salt, baking powder and cinnamon. Add to first mixture and blend. Add nuts. Bake in two greased 9x5 pans at 325° for 1 hour. Remove from pan at once.

### Flossie's Thanksgiving Dressing

1 small cake of cornbread
12-14 biscuits (day old)
1 large pkg. Pepperidge Farm®
   Herb Dressing Mix

1 cup chopped onion
Salt and pepper to taste
1 tablespoon sage
Chicken broth to moisten

Combine ingredients. Spread in 9x15x1" greased pan. Dot with butter. Bake at 450° until golden brown.

Notes:

## Jane's Rice

1 stick margarine, melted
1 cup rice
1 can mushrooms, juice and all

1 can onion soup
¾ cup water
1 can water chestnuts, sliced

Brown rice in margarine and pour into a casserole dish. Add remaining ingredients and cover. Cook 1 hour at 350°.

## Junior Johnson's Race Day Biscuits

⅓ cup shortening
⅔ to ¾ cup milk

2 cups self-rising flour

Thoroughly cut shortening into flour. Stir in just enough milk so dough leaves side of bowl and turns into a ball. Knead dough about 10 times on lightly floured surface and pat or roll it ½" thick. Cut with biscuit cutter. Bake 10 to 12 minutes at 450° on ungreased cookie sheet until golden brown. Makes 7-16 biscuits.

## Macaroni and Tomatoes

2 cups uncooked macaroni
1 qt. can tomatoes, cut up fine

1 lb. sausage, cooked, drained

Cook macaroni by package directions. Salt and pepper to taste. Mix macaroni, tomatoes, and sausage. Pour into casserole dish and bake for 40 minutes at 400°.

*"We are the memories we keep in our hearts"*

## Hot Mexican Corn Bread

1 cup self-rising corn meal
¼ teaspoon red pepper
½ cup green pepper, chopped
¼ cup oil
2 eggs, beaten
¼ teaspoon salt
½ cup onion, chopped
½ cup (2 oz) shredded cheese
1 cup milk
1 cup cream style corn

Mix corn meal, red and green peppers. Add remaining ingredients. Bake in greased pan at 450° for 20-25 minutes. Serve warm or cool.

*Variation:* Add **1 cup sour cream** and **1 to 1½ cup cheddar cheese** to recipe. Combine all ingredients except cheese. Pour half mixture in pan. Put cheese on top. Top off with remaining batter. Bake at 350° for 45-55 minutes.

## Mexican Corn Bread

2 med. jalapeno peppers, seeded and chopped
1 box Jiffy® corn muffin mix
1½ cups shredded cheddar cheese
1 large onion, chopped
3 eggs, slightly beaten
2½ cups milk
1½ cups self-rising corn meal
1 (8 oz) can cream corn
½ cup vegetable oil

Combine ingredients in large bowl. Pour into greased 9x13" pan and bake at 400° for 40 minutes or until done.

**Notes:**

## Orange Muffins

1½ cups sugar  
½ cup dark corn syrup  

Juice from 2 oranges

Combine the above ingredients. Let stand for at least 2 hours. (This mixture is for dipping the muffins).

1 cup butter  
1 cup sugar  
2 eggs  
¾ cup buttermilk  
3 cups flour  

1 teaspoon baking powder  
1 teaspoon soda  
1 teaspoon vanilla  
Juice and rind of 2 oranges  
½ cup raisins (ground)

Cream butter, sugar and eggs. Add alternately buttermilk, flour, baking powder and soda mixture. Then add vanilla, juice and raisins. Bake at 400° for 10-20 minutes. Don't get too brown. While muffins are hot, dip in first mixture and dry on waxed paper. Keep in covered container to keep moist.

## Quick Cheese Grits

2⅔ cups hot water  
¾ teaspoon salt  
1 cup (4 oz) shredded cheddar cheese  

⅔ cup quick-cooking grits  
1 tablespoon butter or margarine

Combine water, grits, and salt in a 2-qt. casserole. Microwave on high for 9 to 10 minutes, stirring after 5 minutes. Add butter and cheese, mixing well. Microwave on high for 1 minute or until butter and cheese melt; stir well.

Notes:

## Quick Banana Bread

½ cup shortening
1 cup sugar
2 eggs
2 bananas

2 cups flour
½ teaspoon baking soda
¼ to ½ cup ground nuts

Cream butter and sugar together. Add eggs and beat well. Add mashed bananas, flour, soda and nuts. Grease and flour two, 4x8 loaf pans. Pour into pans and bake at 350° for 45-50 minutes or until toothpick comes out clean when center is tested. Makes 2 loaves.

## Whole Wheat Muffins

1⅔ cups sifted whole wheat flour
2 teaspoons baking powder
A scant ½ teaspoon salt

1 egg
⅓ cup oil
¾ cup milk (or 1 cup buttermilk)

Mix flour, baking powder, and salt. Set aside. In separate bowl, beat milk, egg, oil and honey. Make a well in dry ingredients and add liquids all at once. Stir only until the flour is moist. Batter will be lumpy. Bake in greased muffin tin at 400° for 25 minutes. Makes 9 muffins.

**Notes:**

# Cakes, Pies and Cookies

*"True Friends visit us in prosperity only when invited, but in adversity, they come without invitation"*

*Cakes, Pies & Cookies* 83

# Cakes

### Flossie's 22-Minute Chocolate Cake

¼ cup cocoa
½ cup salad oil
2 cups self-rising flour
1 teaspoon soda
½ cup buttermilk

1 stick margarine
1 cup water
2 cups sugar
2 eggs, slightly beaten

Mix cocoa, margarine, salad oil and water and bring to a boil. Sift and mix flour, soda, and sugar. Pour over liquid mixture. Add eggs and buttermilk. Bake at 400° for 22 minutes or until done in a 9x13-inch pan.

*Icing*

3 tablespoons cocoa
½ stick margarine
½ cup black walnuts

4 to 5 tablespoons milk
1 box powdered sugar

Bring first three ingredients to a boil. Add powdered sugar until it is of spreading consistency. Sprinkle cake with nuts then spread on frosting.

**Notes:**

## Admonition Coconut Cake
*A four day cake that's worth the wait!*

2 cups sugar
2 (6 oz) pkg. frozen coconut
2 cups sour cream

1 (2-layer size) pkg. yellow cake mix

The night before baking, combine sugar, sour cream and coconut. Refrigerate.

The next morning, prepare the cake and bake in two layers by package directions. Turn out layers. Cool. Spilt each layer into two layers to make a total of four. Fill and frost with sour cream mixture. Refrigerate. Do not cut for four days.

## Apple Nut Cake

Mix together **2 cups sugar, 3 eggs** and **1½ cups oil**. Set aside.

3 cups flour
1 teaspoon salt
3 cups finely diced raw apples
1 teaspoon cinnamon

1 teaspoon soda (heaping)
1 tablespoon vanilla
1 (16 oz) frozen coconut
1 cup pecans

Sift flour, salt, soda, and cinnamon. Mix with first batter. Add apples, vanilla, coconut, and pecans. Grease and flour Bundt® or tube pan. Bake at 325° for 1 hour and 30 minutes. Let stand 20 minutes before removing from pan.

**Notes:**

# Cakes, Pies & Cookies

## Basic Chocolate Cake

2¾ cups unsifted cake flour
½ cup cocoa
1½ teaspoons baking soda
½ teaspoon salt
1 cup butter or margarine, softened

2 cups sugar
3 eggs
1½ teaspoons vanilla
1½ cups ice water

In medium bowl, stir together flour, cocoa, baking soda and salt. Set aside. In large bowl, cream butter and sugar. Add eggs, one at a time. Add vanilla and continue beating. Add ice water and flour mixture alternately. Blend until smooth. *This recipe is good for layers or 9x13" pan.* Grease and flour pans. Bake at 350° for 25-30 minutes in 3 (9") layers, or bake at 350° at 30-35 minutes in 9x13" pan.

## Boiled Raisin Cake

2 cups sugar
2 cups hot water
½ cup lard
½ cup butter
2 teaspoons baking soda
1 cup chopped nuts

1 lb. seeded muscat raisins
   (cut in small pieces)
2 teaspoons cinnamon
2 teaspoons cloves
1 teaspoon salt
3½ cups flour

Put all ingredients in large kettle except baking soda, flour and nuts. Boil one-minute. Remove from heat and add baking soda at once, beating hard. When batter is completely cool, add flour and chopped nuts.

Grease and flour Bundt® or tube pan carefully as this cake is easy to stick to pan. Bake ½ hour at 350°, then 1½ hours at 325°. This recipe is over 100 years old and was used at Christmas for fruitcake.

**Notes:**

## Buttermilk-Chocolate Pudding Cake

2 cups sugar
2 eggs, beaten
½ teaspoon salt
¼ cup cocoa
1 cup water
Buttermilk-chocolate frosting (see below)

1 cup salad oil
2 cups all-purpose flour
1 teaspoon soda
½ cup buttermilk
1 teaspoon vanilla extract

Combine sugar, oil and eggs. Beat well. Combine dry ingredients. Add to sugar mixture, a small amount at a time, stirring well after each addition. Blend in buttermilk, water and vanilla. The batter will be thin.

Spoon batter into a lightly greased 13x9x2-inch pan. Bake at 350° for 25 minutes. **Prepare buttermilk-chocolate frosting.** Spread frosting over hot cake, and allow to cool in pan. Cut into squares to serve.

## Buttermilk-Chocolate Frosting

1 (16 oz) pkg. powdered sugar
¼ cup butter or margarine, melted
⅓ cup buttermilk

¼ cup cocoa
1 teaspoon vanilla extract

Combine sugar and cocoa. Blend well. Stir in remaining ingredients.

**Notes:**

### Best Yet Pineapple Cake

3 baked layers of yellow cake
1 stick butter at room temperature
1 pkg. (3 oz) cream cheese
(8 oz) sour cream
1 cup granulated sugar
1 carton (8 oz) whipped topping
1 can (20 oz) crushed pineapple, undrained
1 pkg. (6 oz) frozen coconut
1 pkg. (4 serving size) instant vanilla pudding mix

Blend together butter, cream cheese, sour cream and sugar. Add pineapple and coconut. Blend. Sprinkle with dry pudding mix as it comes in the package. Fold in whipped topping. Use to fill and frost layers of yellow cake.

### Blueberry Nut Crunch

1 can (2½) crushed pineapple
2 cups blueberries
1 box yellow cake mix
1 cup pecans, chopped
1 cup sugar (divided into a ¾ cup and and ¼ cup)
½ cup butter, melted

Lightly grease 13x9" pan. Spread undrained pineapple over bottom of pan. Add layer of blueberries and sprinkle on ¾ cup sugar. Spread dry cake mix over all. Drizzle melted butter over cake. Top with nuts and sprinkle remaining ¼ cup sugar. Bake at 350° for 25 minutes. Take from oven. Cut down to bottom of pan to let juice rise. Return to oven and bake 10-15 minutes longer.

**Notes:**

## White Wine Cake

1 box Duncan Hines® Deluxe Cake Mix
1 (3½ oz) box instant vanilla pudding
4 tablespoons white sugar
4 tablespoons brown sugar
4 eggs
2 teaspoons cinnamon
¾ cup oil
¾ cup water
½ cup white wine

Mix dry ingredients. Add remaining ingredients and mix until smooth. Pour mix into greased tube or bundt® pan. Bake at 325° for 60 minutes.

*Glaze:*

½ cup white sugar
¼ cup white wine
½ stick butter or margarine

Mix ingredients. Bring to boil. Pour mixture over White Wine Cake. Let stand for 1 hour before turning out of pan.

**Notes:**

## Deluxe Carrot Cake

2 cups sifted plain flour
2 teaspoons baking powder
1½ teaspoons baking soda
1 teaspoon salt
2 teaspoons cinnamon
2 cups sugar

1½ cups salad oil
4 eggs
2 cups finely grated carrots (4 large)
1 can crushed pineapple, drained
½ cup chopped nuts
1 can coconut

Sift the first five ingredients together then add sugar, oil and eggs. Mix well. Blend in thoroughly carrots, pineapple, nuts and coconuts. Pour mixture in three, greased and floured 9-inch round layers. Bake at 350° for 35 minutes. When cool, spread with Cream Cheese Frosting (see below).

## Cream Cheese Frosting
*(For Deluxe Carrot Cake)*

½ cup butter
1 (8 oz) pkg. cream cheese

1 lb. powdered sugar
1 teaspoon vanilla

Cream together in order listed. Spread over cake.

**Notes:**

## Champagne Cake

1 white cake mix
1 cup club soda
½ cup oil
1 large can crushed pineapple, drained

1 pkg. pistachio instant pudding
4 large eggs
1 small jar red cherries, drained, chopped
½ cup pecans

Combine cake mix, pudding, club soda, eggs and oil. Beat with mixer. Stir in remaining ingredients with spoon. Bake at 350° for 20 minutes. Makes 3 layers.

*Icing:* Mix **1 cup pecans, ¾ stick margarine, 1 box powdered sugar, 6 oz. coconut, 1 (8 oz) cream cheese and 2 tablespoons vanilla.**

**Notes:**

# Cakes, Pies & Cookies

## Cherry Pound Cake

1½ cups Crisco®  
3 cups sugar  
6 eggs  
1 cup milk  

3¾ cups plain flour  
½ cup chopped maraschino cherries  
1 teaspoon vanilla flavoring  

Cream shortening. Add sugar gradually, beating well. Beat in eggs one at a time. Add vanilla. Add milk and flour alternately. Stir in chopped cherries. Bake in tube pan for 1½ hours at 300°. Frost with Cherry Pound Cake Frosting. (See below).

## Cherry Pound Cake Frosting

1 small pkg. cream cheese  
½ stick margarine  
1 box powdered sugar  
¼ cup cherry juice  

½ cup chopped cherries  
½ cup chopped nuts  
½ cup coconut  

Mix and frost cooled cake.

## Chess Cake

1 box yellow cake mix  
3 eggs  
1 stick margarine  

1 (8 oz) pkg. cream cheese  
1 box powdered sugar  

Mix cake mix, 1 egg, and margarine, pat into bottom of 9x13-inch pan. Mix cream cheese, 2 eggs and powdered sugar. Pour over other mixture. Bake for 30 minutes at 350°.

**Notes:**

## Chocolate Pound Cake

2 sticks butter (or 1 butter and 1 margarine)
½ cup vegetable shortening
3 cups sugar
3 cups flour
5 eggs
½ teaspoon salt
½ teaspoon baking powder
½ cup cocoa
1 cup milk
2 teaspoon vanilla (added to milk)
4 tablespoons milk

Cream butter and sugar. Add eggs one at a time. Heat four tablespoons of milk. Add to sugar and butter mixture. Sift dry ingredients three times. Add to mixture. Bake at 350° for 1 hr. 20 mins.

## Chocolate Chip Pound Cake

1 box yellow cake mix
1 box instant chocolate pudding
¾ cup water
4 large eggs
1 cup sour cream
1 small pkg. chocolate chips
¾ cup oil

Sift together cake mix and chocolate pudding. Make well in center of dry ingredients. Add remaining ingredients except chocolate chips. Beat well. Stir in chocolate chips with spatula. Pour batter in tube pan and bake 55 minutes to 1 hour at 350°. Cool on wire rack.

**Notes:**

## Crusty Pound Cake

2 sticks margarine
½ cup Crisco®
3 cups sugar
5 eggs

3 cups flour
1 cup milk
1 teaspoon vanilla
1 teaspoon lemon flavoring

Cream margarine, shortening and sugar. Add eggs, one at a time, beating well after each. Add flavorings. Then add flour alternately with milk, mixing thoroughly. **Start in cold oven.** Bake at 300° for 1½ hours. **Do not open door.**

*"God often allows our hearts to be broken, so that he can beautify our souls"*

Notes:

## Fresh Coconut Pound Cake

1 cup butter, softened
3 cups sugar
6 eggs
3 cups all-purpose flour
¼ teaspoon baking soda

¼ teaspoon salt
1 (8 oz) carton dairy sour cream
1 cup fresh coconut
1 teaspoon vanilla extract
1 teaspoon coconut extract

Cream butter, gradually adding sugar. Beat until light and fluffy. Add one egg at a time, beating well after each addition. In separate bowl, combine flour, baking soda and salt. Mix well. Add sour cream to mixture. Stir in coconut and extracts. Pour batter into greased and floured 10" tube pan. Bake at 350° for 1 hour and 20 minutes, or until a wooden pick inserted in center comes out clean. Cool in pan 10-15 minutes. Remove from pan and cool completely before icing or cutting.

*Icing:*

½ cup vegetable shortening
1 box (1 lb) confectioner's sugar
1 teaspoon vanilla (preferably clear)

¼ cup water
⅛ teaspoon salt

Combine ingredients in large bowl. Mix with electric mixer on high speed until fluffy. Frost top and sides of Coconut Pound Cake.

**Notes:**

## Diamond Jubilee Applesauce Cake

2½ cups sifted flour
¼ teaspoon baking powder
1½ teaspoon salt
½ teaspoon cloves
½ cup soft shortening
1½ cups unsweetened applesauce
½ cup chopped nuts

2 cups sugar
1½ teaspoon soda
¾ teaspoon cinnamon
½ teaspoon allspice
½ cup water
2 eggs
1 cup raisins, cut up

Sift dry ingredients together. Add shortening, water and applesauce. Beat 2 minutes using medium speed. Scrape sides and bottom of bowl constantly. Add eggs. Beat 2 more minutes, scraping bowl constantly. Fold in nuts and raisins. Pour in 2-layer pans (9x1½"). Bake in preheated 350° oven for 35 to 50 minutes. Cool.

## Fruit Cocktail Cake

1½ cups white sugar
¼ cup Wesson® oil
2¼ cups plain flour
½ teaspoon salt

2 teaspoon baking soda
2 eggs
2 teaspoon vanilla
1 can (16 oz) fruit cocktail (save juice)

Beat eggs. Add sugar, oil and vanilla. Mix soda, salt and flour. Stir in fruit cocktail including juice. Bake in a 13x9x2-inch greased pan for 35 minutes at 350° or 325° for 45 to 50 minutes.

For topping, mix together **1 stick margarine, 1 cup sugar, 1 small can evaporated milk, and 1 small can coconut.** Boil for 10 minutes, stirring constantly. Pour over cake while hot. **Chopped nuts** can be added to the topping.

**Notes:**

### German Chocolate Cream Cheese Cake

1 box German chocolate cake mix (with oil)
1 box powdered sugar
1 (8 oz) cream cheese
1 stick margarine, melted
1 cup nuts

Grease and flour pan (9x13-inches). Mix cake by directions on box. Put chopped nuts in bottom of pan, followed by cake batter. Cream butter, cheese and sugar together and pour on top of mix before baking. May have to drop cheese mixture by spoonfuls if too thick. Bake at 350° for 45 minutes.

### German Chocolate Upside Down Cake

1 cup pecans, chopped
1 box German chocolate cake mix
1 pkg. (8 oz) cream cheese
1 cup coconut
1 cup (2 sticks) melted margarine
1 lb. confectioner's sugar

Mix pecans and coconut together and spread on bottom of a well-greased 9x13" pan. Mix cake mix according to the directions on box. Spread mixture over the nuts and coconut mixture. Mix the margarine, cream cheese and confectioner's sugar until smooth. Spread over cake mix layer, leaving about 1 inch margin from sides of pan. Bake at 350° for 50 minutes.

**Notes:**

## Honeybun Cake

1 box yellow cake mix  
¾ cup Wesson® oil  

4 eggs  
1 cup sour cream (8 oz)  

Blend these ingredients to form a batter. Pour half of batter into greased and floured 9x13x2-inch pan. Sprinkle a dry mixture of **1 cup brown sugar, 1½ tablespoons cinnamon, and 1½ cups chopped nuts or raisins** on top of batter. Pour rest of batter into pan and rest of dry mixture on top.

Swirl dry mixture into batter (as for a marble cake). Bake for 45 minutes to 1 hour at 275°-300°.

Prepare a glaze of **2 cups powdered sugar, ½ teaspoon vanilla** and **4 tablespoons milk**. Pour over *hot* cake.

## Lemon Pound Cake

1 stick margarine  
1 cup Crisco®  
2⅔ cups sugar  

3 cups flour  
¼ teaspoon salt  
1 cup milk  

Mix above ingredients until light and fluffy. Blend **1 teaspoon baking powder** and **2½ tablespoons lemon flavoring**. Add **5 eggs**, one at a time, mixing after each until blended. *Keep all ingredients at room temperature.* Pour into large tube pan which has been greased and floured. Bake at 325° for 1 hour and 20 minutes. As soon as you take the cake out of the oven, run a knife around the sides, and return to rack of oven for about five minutes. Loosen the sides from the pan, turn out on a plate, and leave uncovered.

**Notes:**

## Lemon Supreme Pound Cake

2 sticks margarine
3 cups sugar
3½ cups sifted flour
¼ teaspoon salt
2 teaspoons lemon flavoring

½ cup vegetable shortening
6 eggs
½ tablespoon baking powder
1 cup milk
1 teaspoon vanilla

Cream margarine, shortening and sugar. Add eggs, one at a time. Add dry ingredients alternately with milk. Add flavoring. Pour into greased and floured 10" tube pan. Bake at 325° for 1 hour, 15 minutes. Remove from oven and let stand 10 minutes.

*Icing:*

1 stick margarine
1 teaspoon lemon flavoring
Several drops yellow food coloring

Dash salt
Juice from ½ lemon (1 tablespoon)
1 box confectioner's sugar

Cream together above ingredients. Add enough **milk** until you reach a good spreading consistency. Spread this icing on cooled cake, then sprinkle can of **coconut** over the icing.

**Notes:**

# Cakes, Pies & Cookies

## Nut Cake

2½ cups flour
1 tablespoon vanilla
1½ qts. pecans
1 teaspoon black walnut flavoring

2 cups sugar
5 eggs
½ lb. butter or margarine

Cream butter and sugar until smooth. Add eggs, one at a time, beating after each is added. Add flavoring, then flour. Mix until smooth. Mix pecans with small amount of flour and fold into batter. Bake in tube or loaf pan for 2 hours at 250°.

*Icing:* Mix ¼ **lb. butter** and **1 box powdered sugar.** Add enough **milk** to spread.

## Oatmeal Cake
### (Very rich!)

1¼ cups boiling water
1 cup quick oats
½ cup vegetable shortening
1 cup brown sugar
1 cup white sugar

2 eggs
1⅓ cups flour
1 teaspoon soda
½ teaspoon cinnamon

Pour water over oats. Set aside. Cream together shortening, and sugars. Add eggs, beating after each addition. Will form a creamy mixture. Sift together flour, soda and cinnamon. Add to creamy mixture gradually. Bake in 9x13" pan at 350° for 45-50 minutes.

*Icing:* Cream together **1 stick butter** and **1 cup brown sugar.** Add **2 egg yolks** and beat well. Stir in **1 cup chopped nuts,** and **1 can angel-flaked coconut.** Add enough **milk** to make mixture spread easily over cake. Ice cake and return to oven, broil for a few minutes until lightly browned.

Notes:

## Old-Fashioned Icebox Fruit Cake

*This is an old recipe and my family's favorite Christmas fruit cake. Cake will weigh between 6 and 7 pounds!*

| | |
|---|---|
| 1½ cups English walnuts | 2 cups pecans |
| ½ lb. Brazil nuts (freeze before cracking) | 1 lb. dark raisins |
| | 1 lb. golden raisins |
| 1 lb. graham crackers | ½ to 1 lb. candied cherries |
| ½ to 1 lb. candied pineapple | 1 lb. marshmallows |
| 1½ cups evaporated milk | |

Line bottom of tube pan with wax paper. Grind everything except pineapples and cherries. Chunk pineapple and leave cherries whole. Melt marshmallows in warm milk over low heat. Fold in ground goodies and put in pineapple and cherries last. Pack firm in cake pan and refrigerate overnight. Remove from cake pan. Remove wax paper from cake and rewrap with plastic or Saran Wrap®. Store in refrigerator until gone.

## Pecan Cake

| | |
|---|---|
| 1 lb. butter | ½ lb. candied pineapple |
| 1 lb. sugar | 6 eggs |
| 1 lb. flour | 1 teaspoon baking powder |
| 1 lb. pecans | ½ teaspoon salt |
| 1 lb. white raisins | 4 teaspoons lemon extract |
| ½ lb. candied cherries | |

Cream butter and sugar. Add beaten eggs. Sift flour with baking powder and salt. Dredge fruit and nuts with ½ cup of the flour. Add lemon extract to the butter mixture, then fold in flour. Add fruits and nuts last. Bake in two loaf pans or tube pan for 3½ hours at 275°.

Notes:

## Pineapple Pound Cake

1 cup vegetable oil
3 cups sugar
6 eggs
3 cups all-purpose flour
1 teaspoon baking powder
pinch of salt
¾ cup of crushed pineapple
1 teaspoon vanilla extract

Combine oil and sugar, mix well. Add eggs one at a time, beating well after each addition. Combine flour, baking powder and salt. Gradually add to oil mixture, beating well. Stir in pineapple and vanilla. Pour batter into well-greased and floured 10-inch tube pan. Bake at 350° for 1 hour and 25 minutes or until done. Invert pan, cool for 15 minutes. Remove from pan and cool completely. Add Pineapple Pound Cake Glaze.

## Pineapple Pound Cake Glaze

2 teaspoon sugar
1½ teaspoon cornstarch
½ cup pineapple juice

Combine sugar and cornstarch in a heavy saucepan. Stir well. Add juice, stirring well. Cook over medium heat until thickened and translucent. Cool. Pour pineapple glaze over cake.

**Notes:**

## Poppy Seed Cake

2 tablespoons sugar
1 teaspoon cinnamon
1 pkg. lemon cake mix
1 teaspoon almond extract
4 eggs
1 small pkg. instant pudding
1 cup orange juice
½ cup oil
¼ cup poppy seeds

Preheat oven to 350°. Mix cinnamon and sugar. Sprinkle into greased bundt® pan. Shake out excess. Combine remaining ingredients into a large mixing bowl. Beat for 5 minutes. Do not underbeat. Batter should be thick and creamy. Pour into pan. Bake for 45 minutes. Remove and cool for 30 minutes. Remove from pan. Cool thoroughly before slicing.

## Pound Cake

2 cups cake flour
¼ teaspoon baking powder
5 eggs
1 cup Crisco®
1 tablespoon vanilla extract
½ tablespoon almond extract
¼ teaspoon salt
3 cups sugar
1 stick butter
1 cup sweet milk
¾ tablespoon lemon extract

Blend dry ingredients, except baking powder, which will be added to last addition of flour. Cream sugar, Crisco® and butter. Add eggs, one at a time, mixing well after each. Add dry ingredients beginning and ending with flour, alternating with milk. Bake at 325° for 1 hour and 15-20 minutes.

Notes:

## "Pole Winning" Pound Cake

3 cups sugar
1 cup Crisco®
½ cup margarine
6 eggs
1 cup milk
3 cups flour
½ teaspoon baking powder
½ teaspoon salt
1 teaspoon lemon flavoring
2 teaspoon vanilla flavoring
1 teaspoon almond flavoring

Cream Crisco,® margarine and sugar. Add eggs one at a time. Mix well. Add milk. Combine flour, salt and baking powder. Add flavoring. Bake at 325° for 1½ hours or until brown.

## Prune Cake with Buttermilk Icing

1½ cups sugar
1 cup vegetable oil
3 eggs
2 cups sifted flour
1 teaspoon soda
1 teaspoon cinnamon
1 teaspoon nutmeg
1 teaspoon allspice
¼ teaspoon salt
1 cup buttermilk
1 teaspoon vanilla
1 cup chopped nuts
1 cup prunes (cooked, seeded, chopped)
1 cup raisins

Blend sugar and oil. Add eggs and mix. Sift dry ingredients together and add alternately with milk. Add vanilla, nuts and prunes. Pour into greased pan 11x7x2 deep and bake at 300° for about 1 hour or until done. When done, remove from oven and *while still hot*, cover with the following:

*Buttermilk Icing:* Boil 1 cup sugar, ½ cup buttermilk, ½ teaspoon baking soda, 1 teaspoon white corn syrup, ¼ cup butter and ½ teaspoon vanilla in deep pan until it forms a soft ball. Pour over hot cake without beating. Leave the cake in the pan until ready to cut into squares for serving.

**Notes:**

### Red Velvet Pound Cake

1 cup softened margarine  
3 cups sugar  
3 cups flour  
½ cup baking cocoa  
1 cup milk  
2 (1 oz) bottled red food coloring  

½ cup shortening  
5 eggs  
¼ teaspoon baking powder  
⅛ teaspoon salt  
1 teaspoon vanilla extract  

Cream margarine, shortening and sugar until light and fluffy. Beat in eggs, one at a time. Combine flour, baking powder, cocoa and salt. Add to creamed mixture alternately with milk. Mix well after each addition. Mix in vanilla and food coloring. Spoon into greased and floured tube pan. Bake at 300° for 1½ hours.

### Red Velvet Pound Cake Frosting

1 cup milk  
2 tablespoons all-purpose flour  
1 teaspoon vanilla  

1 cup margarine, softened  
1 cup granulated sugar  

Combine milk and flour in saucepan. Cook and stir constantly over medium high heat until boiling. Reduce heat to low and cook 2 minutes longer. Cool. Set aside. In small mixing bowl, cream margarine and sugar until very light and fluffy. Add cooled milk mixture and beat until frosting has appearance of whipped cream. Add vanilla. Mix well.

**Notes:**

# Cakes, Pies & Cookies

## Punch Bowl Cake

1 box yellow cake mix
2 boxes vanilla pudding
    (not instant)
1 cup chopped pecans

2 cans cherry pie filling
3 small cans crushed pineapple
1 large container Cool Whip®

Bake cake as directed on box, in two layers. Break one layer in small pieces and place in bottom of punch bowl. Mix pudding as directed on box, and pour half over cake while pudding is hot. Add a layer of cherries. Add 1 can of crushed pineapples. Add Cool Whip.® Sprinkle with nuts. Repeat all of the above using remaining ingredients.

## Scotch Chocolate Cake

2 cups all-purpose flour
1 stick margarine
4 heaping tablespoons cocoa
½ cup buttermilk
2 eggs

2 cups granulated sugar
½ cup vegetable shortening
1 cup water
1 teaspoon soda
1 teaspoon vanilla

Combine flour and sugar in mixing bowl, mixing well. In saucepan, put margarine, shortening, cocoa and water, bring to a rapid boil, and pour over flour and sugar, mixing gradually. Put soda in buttermilk and add with other ingredients. Mix and turn into a greased and floured pan. Bake at 400° for 30 minutes or until done. *Make icing 5 minutes before cake is done and pour hot icing over hot cake.*

*Icing:* Combine **1 stick margarine, 4 tablespoons cocoa** and **6 tablespoons milk** in saucepan. Bring to a boil, stirring constantly to prevent sticking. Remove from heat and pour over hot cake.

**Notes:**

## Sour Cream Coffee Cake

Cream together **1 stick margarine** and **1 cup sugar**. Add **2 cups flour, 1 teaspoon baking powder, 1 teaspoon baking soda** and **1 cup sour cream**. Batter will be stiff.

Grease 2 (9") pans or 1 (9x13") pan. Place batter in pan. Combine the following ingredients and sprinkle over batter:

½ **cup brown sugar**
½ **cup chopped walnuts**
3 tablespoons melted margarine or butter

½ **teaspoon cinnamon**
¼ **teaspoon vanilla**

Bake in 350° oven for 25 minutes. When cool, drizzle a little powdered sugar icing over top, if desired.

**Notes:**

# Cakes, Pies & Cookies

## Strawberry Kringle Cake

2 teaspoons strawberry gelatin
1½ cups sugar
12 oz. sour cream
Whipped cream

¼ cup boiling water
1½ cups strawberries, mashed
1 pkg. (2 layer) white or yellow cake mix

Dissolve gelatin in boiling water. Cool. Add sugar and stir until dissolved. Gently stir in strawberries and sour cream. Refrigerate overnight. Bake cake mix according to directions on box. Cool. Split layers into 4 layers. Put layers together with container in refrigerator. Chill 3 to 4 days. About 1 hour before serving, frost entire cake with whipped cream. Garnish with fresh strawberries.

## Sweet Potato Cake

1½ cups cooking oil
4 eggs, separated
2½ cups sifted cake flour
¼ teaspoon salt
1 teaspoon nutmeg
1 cup chopped nuts

2 cups sugar
4 teaspoons hot water
3 teaspoons baking powder
1 teaspoon cinnamon
1½ cups grated raw sweet potatoes
1 teaspoon vanilla

Beat oil and sugar together until smooth. Add egg yolks and beat well. Add water, then dry ingredients sifted together. Stir in potatoes, nuts, vanilla, and beat well. Beat egg whites until stiff and fold into mixture. Bake in greased, 8-inch layer (or loaf pans) at 350° for 25 to 30 minutes. Cool and frost.

*Frosting:* Combine **1 large can evaporated milk, 1 stick margarine, 1 teaspoon vanilla, 1 cup sugar** and **3 egg yolks** in sauce pan. Cook for 12 minutes over low heat, stirring constantly until thick. Remove from heat and add **1¼ cups flaked coconut.** Beat until cool and of spreading consistency.

**Notes:**

## Toasted Butter Pecan Cake

| | |
|---|---|
| 2 cups chopped pecans | 2½ sticks margarine |
| 2 cups sugar | 4 eggs |
| 3 cups sifted flour | 2 teaspoons baking powder |
| 2 teaspoons vanilla | 1 cup milk |

In a shallow baking pan, toast pecans in ½ stick margarine in a moderate oven. Stir to prevent burning. Remove from oven and allow to cool. Cream 2 sticks margarine and sugar together. Add eggs one at a time, beating well after each. Sift together flour and baking powder and add to creamed mixture, alternating with vanilla and milk. Add 1 ½ cups of the pecans (the rest will go on frosting). Turn into 3 greased and floured layer cake pans. Bake at 350° for 25-30 minutes or until done. Turn out on racks to cool.

*Frosting:*

| | |
|---|---|
| ½ stick margarine | 1 box powdered sugar |
| 1 tablespoon vanilla | Evaporated milk |

Heat margarine in heavy pan until a little darker than golden. Remove from heat. Gradually blend in part of sugar. Add evaporated milk gradually as needed, to make mixture of proper spreading consistency. Add remaining ½ cup of pecans.

*"A Friend loves at all times"*

Notes:

# Pies

### Flossie's Chocolate Pie

3 cups sugar
4 eggs, beaten
7 tablespoons cocoa
1 teaspoon vanilla
1 cup chopped pecans

1 stick margarine, melted
1 tall can Pet® Milk
Pinch of salt
2 cups coconut

Mix and pour into 3 unbaked pie shells. Bake at 450° for 40-45 minutes.

### Chocolate Pie

2 eggs, separated
1 cup sugar
4 tablespoons flour
4 tablespoons cocoa

1/8 teaspoon salt
2 cups milk
2 tablespoons butter
1 teaspoon vanilla

Heat milk in double boiler. Mix sugar, flour, cocoa and salt. Beat egg yolks and add dry ingredients along with 1/2 cup of warm milk. Add to rest of milk in double boiler and cook until thick. Add butter. Cool. Then add vanilla. Pour in baked pie shell.

*"Drive with care, Life has no spare"*

Notes:

## Coconut Cream Pie

5 egg yolks, beaten
5 tablespoons flour
1 teaspoon vanilla
½ stick butter or margarine

1½ cups sugar
1 cup angel-flaked coconut
3 cups milk
2 (8") pie shells, baked

Mix together flour and sugar. Add egg yolks, milk, and butter. Heat in the top of a double boiler over hot water, cooking and stirring until thickened. Add vanilla and coconut. Cool.

*Meringue:* Beat 5 egg whites until stiff. Gradually add 10 tablespoons sugar and beat well. Pour the coconut mixture into the baked pie shells and cover with meringue. Brown at 350°. Refrigerate.

## Coconut Cream Pie

½ cup sugar
¼ teaspoon salt
1 cup coconut
2 teaspoon vanilla
1 baked (9") pie shell

½ cup sifted flour
3 cups milk
2 egg yolks, slightly beaten
1 tablespoon butter

Combine sugar, flour and salt in double boiler, add milk and stir until smooth. Add coconut. Cook 15 minutes, stir constantly. Mix small amount with egg yolks. Return to double boiler and cook 2 minutes. Add vanilla and butter. Cook before putting in pie shell.

**Notes:**

### Coconut Pecan Pie

5 eggs, beaten
1 stick margarine, melted
1 teaspoon vanilla flavoring
1 cup pecans, chopped

2 cups sugar
1 tablespoon lemon juice
1½ cups coconut, packed
2 (9") unbaked pie shells

Thoroughly combine eggs, sugar, margarine, lemon juice and vanilla. Stir in coconut and pecans. Pour into unbaked pie shells. Bake at 350° in oven 45 to 50 minutes. Makes 2 pies.

### Coconut Praline Pie

2 (9") pie shells, baked
¼ cup melted butter

1 cup coconut, toasted
1 cup chopped pecans

Cook above ingredients on low. Set aside to cool.

Cream together **1 can Eagle Brand® Milk** and **1 (8 oz) cream cheese,** softened. Add **6 oz. Cool Whip.®** Put in baked crust. Cover with coconut mixture. Drizzle **caramel ice cream topping** over. Chill.

Notes:

## Creamy Praline Pie

2 or 3 frozen pie shells or
   graham cracker crusts
7 oz. flaked coconut
8 oz. cream cheese
12 oz. butterscotch or caramel ice cream topping
1 cup chopped pecans
1 can sweetened condensed milk
16 oz. Cool Whip®
¼ cup margarine

Bake two deep dish or three thin pie shells according to directions.

Toast pecans, coconut and margarine in oven on broil. Watch carefully and don't burn.

Pour sweetened condensed milk into large mixing bowl. Add softened cream cheese, beat until smooth and fold in Cool Whip.® Take cool pie shells and layer as follows: cream cheese mixture, toasted pecans and coconut, drizzle with ice cream topping. Layer twice. Freeze pies. Can be slightly thawed or eaten frozen.

**Notes:**

## Peach Pie

1 heaping cup plain flour
1 stick margarine

3 tablespoons powdered sugar

Press above ingredients in deep dish pie pan. Bake at 350° and cool. Beat **8 oz. cream cheese** and **½ cup sugar** with mixer and pour in pie crust. Pour **4 cups peaches** over mixture. Set aside.

Bring **1 cup sugar, 3 tablespoons cornstarch, 3 tablespoons peach Jello®** and **1 cup water** to a boil. Let cool. Pour over peaches.

## Derby Pie

1 stick margarine
4 eggs
1 cup coconut
1 cup chocolate chips

1½ cups sugar
1 teaspoon vanilla
1 cup chopped pecans
2 pie crusts

Melt margarine and add other ingredients. Mix and pour into pie crusts. Bake at 325° for 35 minutes.

## Different Pecan Pie

3 egg whites, beaten
1 cup sugar
1 teaspoon baking powder

1 cup graham cracker crumbs
1 cup chopped pecans

Beat egg whites until stiff. Beat in sugar and baking powder. Stir in graham cracker crumbs and pecans. Pour into a greased pan or 9-inch pyrex® dish and bake at 350° for 30 minutes. *Serve topped with whipped cream and shaved chocolate if desired.*

**Notes:**

### Egg Custard Pie

4 eggs
¾ cup sugar
1½ cups milk
Dash of salt
2½ teaspoons vanilla flavoring
Nutmeg

Beat eggs with salt. Add sugar. Stir. Add milk and vanilla. Mix well. Pour into unbaked pie shell. Sprinkle with nutmeg. Bake at 325° until set. It will take at least one hour.

### Japanese Fruit Pie

2 sticks margarine, melted
2 tablespoons vinegar
1 cup pecans, chopped
1 cup raisins
2 cups sugar
4 eggs, beaten
1 cup coconut

Mix well and pour into 2 unbaked pie shells. Bake at 325° for 40-50 minutes.

### Lemon Chess Pie

2 unbaked pie shells
1 cup sugar
1 stick melted margarine
¼ cup lemon juice
1 tablespoon flour
4 eggs
½ cup milk

Combine sugar and flour in large bowl. Toss lightly with fork to mix. Add eggs, melted margarine, milk, and lemon juice. Beat until smooth. Pour into pie shells. Bake at 350° for 45 to 60 minutes or until golden brown.

**Notes:**

## Lemon Pie

1½ cups water
1¼ cups sugar
3 eggs, separated
6 tablespoons cornstarch

1 tablespoon butter
5 tablespoons lemon juice
2 teaspoons lemon rind
⅛ teaspoon salt

Combine sugar, salt, cornstarch and lemon rind in top of double boiler. Stir in water and cook until thick, stirring constantly. In separate bowl, add a little hot mixture to beaten egg yolks. Pour back into double boiler and cook 2 more minutes. Take from heat. Add butter and lemon juice. Pour into baked pie shell and cover with meringue made from 3 egg whites and 6 tablespoons sugar. Bake at 375° until meringue is golden brown.

## Million Dollar Pie

1 cup Eagle Brand® condensed milk
1 (15 oz) can peaches
1 can mandarin oranges

1 (15 oz) can crushed pineapple
¼ cup lemon juice
1 large container Cool Whip®

Drain peaches, oranges and pineapples. Mix with other ingredients and put into graham cracker crusts. Makes 2 pies.

**Notes:**

## Millionaire's Pie

2 (9-inch) graham cracker crusts
1 (2½) can peach slices
1 (15 oz) can crushed pineapple
1 (8 oz) ctn. frozen whipped topping
Chopped pecans
½ cup lemon juice
1 (15 oz) can sweetened condensed milk

Drain peaches and chop. Combine with drained pineapple and remaining ingredients. Put into crumb crusts. Sprinkle with pecans, if desired. Chill. Makes 2 pies.

## No Crust Apple Pie

1 stick butter
½ cup flour
Milk
1 cup sugar
2 eggs
5 to 6 apples, peeled and sliced

Melt butter in medium-sized casserole. Slice apples and place in butter. Mix sugar, flour, eggs and milk (use enough milk to make this rather thin). Pour over apples and bake at 325° to 350° for about 1 hour or until done. *If you like, before baking, sprinkle with cinnamon.* Eat warm.

## No Bake Lemon Pie

1 (6 oz) can frozen lemonade
1 (9 oz) container Cool Whip®
1 (14 oz) can Eagle Brand® milk
2 graham cracker crusts or frozen pie shells

Mix ingredients well and put into pie shells. Refrigerate.

**Notes:**

## Old-Fashioned Apple Pie

1½ cups chopped apples  
¾ cup sugar  
¾ stick margarine, melted  
1 tablespoon flour  
1 egg, well-beaten  
1 teaspoon cinnamon  
Pinch of salt  
1 unbaked pie shell  

Chop apples and put in unbaked pie shell. Mix remaining ingredients and pour over apples. Bake at 350° until apples are done, about 45 to 50 minutes.

## Peach Custard Pie

1 (9") unbaked pie shell  
1 cup sugar  
3 tablespoons melted margarine  
Sliced fresh peaches  
2 tablespoons flour  
2 eggs  
¼ teaspoon almond extract  

Blend flour and sugar and add to beaten eggs. Blend in melted margarine and almond extract. Fill unbaked pie shell with sliced peaches. Pour sugar mixture over the top. Bake at 450° for 10 minutes. Reduce heat to 350° for 30 minutes longer.

## Pecan Pie

6 eggs  
⅔ teaspoon salt  
1 pt. dark Karo® syrup  
1⅓ cups sugar  
⅔ cup melted butter  

Beat together above ingredients with rotary beater. Mix in **2 cups pecans.** Pour into pastry-lined pan. Bake until set and pastry is nicely browned. Cool. Bake about 35 minutes at 375°. Makes 3 pies.

**Notes:**

## Perfect Pumpkin Pie

1 cup brown sugar
1 tablespoon flour
1 tablespoon cinnamon &
    spice mixed
2 cups cooked pumpkin
1 can evaporated milk
2 pie shells, unbaked

Mix ingredients and pour into pie shells. Bake in preheated oven at 375° for 40 to 45 minutes. Serve plain or top with whipped cream.

## Prize-Winning Pumpkin Pie

2 tablespoons flour
1½ cups cooked pumpkin,
    drained
1 cup undiluted evaporated milk
1¼ cups sugar
½ stick margarine, melted
1 large egg
1 (9") unbaked pie shell

Sift together dry ingredients. Combine dry ingredients with remaining ingredients, in blender of food processor. Mix thoroughly. Pour into unbaked pie shell. Bake in a 425° oven for 8 minutes. Reduce temperature to 350° and bake 45 minutes longer or until almost firm. DO NOT OVERBAKE.

Note: For pies that are less deep, pour filling into 2 unbaked pie shells. Bake at 425° for 8 minutes and then at 350° for 30 minutes or until desired degree of doneness.

Notes:

## Betty's Hospitality Pie

3 pie shells, baked, cooled
1 stick margarine
1 cup sliced almonds
2 cups coconut
1 can (14½ oz) sweetened, condensed milk, *not* evaporated
1 pkg. (8 oz) cream cheese, softened
(16 oz) frozen whipped topping, thawed
Caramel or butterscotch ice cream topping

Mix margarine, almonds and coconut in shallow baking pan. Toast, stirring, in a 350° oven until golden brown; watch to prevent burning. Remove from oven. Cool. Combine and blend together condensed milk and cream cheese. Fold in whipped topping. Put half of the cream cheese mixture in pie shells, dividing equally. Sprinkle with coconut mixture. Drizzle with ice cream topping. Repeat the three layers. Keep refrigerated.

## Grandma's Pumpkin Pie

1 9" unbaked pie shell
2 eggs, slightly beaten
1 (16 oz) can pumpkin
¾ cup sugar
½ teaspoon salt
1½ teaspoons pumpkin pie spice
1⅔ cups evaporated milk

Preheat oven to 400°. Blend all ingredients, stirring well. Pour into pie shell. Bake in center of oven 45-50 minutes.

**Notes:**

### Julie's Black and White Cream Cheese Dessert

*Bottom Layer:*

1 cup chopped pecans
1 cup flour
¼ cup brown sugar
1 stick margarine

*Second Layer:*

1 (8 oz) pkg. cream cheese
1 cup Cool Whip®
1 cup confectioner's sugar

*Third Layer:*

1 pkg. instant chocolate pudding mix
1 pkg. instant vanilla pudding mix
2 cups milk

*Fourth Layer:*

Remainder of (8 oz) carton Cool Whip®
Grated Chocolate

Combine ingredients for bottom layer and mash down in large baking dish. Bake at 350° for 20 minutes. Whip ingredients for layer two and spread over cool crust. Mix layer three ingredients until thickened. Spread over layer two. Top with remaining Cool Whip® and grated chocolate. Refrigerate and serve.

Notes:

# Cakes, Pies & Cookies

## Scotch Apple Pie

5 cups thinly sliced tart apples (4 med.)
1 tablespoon lemon juice
2 tablespoons sugar
1 teaspoon vanilla
Pastry for 9" pie shell
1 cup brown sugar
¼ cup water
¾ cup all-purpose flour
¾ teaspoon salt
3 tablespoons butter or margarine

Combine apples, brown sugar, water and lemon juice in a saucepan. Cover and cook over medium heat until the apples are just tender, about 5 minutes. Mix flour, sugar and salt. Stir into apple mixture. Cook, stirring constantly, until the syrup thickens, about 2 minutes. Remove from heat and stir in vanilla and butter. Bake in a 425° oven about 40-45 minutes or until crust is brown.

## Sour Cream Pecan Pie

3 eggs
½ cup sour cream
½ cup Karo® syrup
1 teaspoon vanilla
1 cup sugar
⅛ teaspoon salt
1 tablespoon butter, melted
1 cup pecans
1 deep dish pie crust

Beat eggs. Add other ingredients, except pecans. Beat until mixed well. Fold in slightly chopped pecans. Pour in pie shells. Bake at 350° for 45 minutes to 1 hour or until knife inserted in middle comes out clean.

Notes:

## Squash Pie

2 cups mashed squash (use blender)  
2 cups sugar  
¾ stick melted butter  
2 tablespoons flour  
3 eggs  
2 tablespoons lemon extract  

Mix flour and sugar. Beat eggs. Add squash to eggs and flour and sugar mixture. Add lemon and melted butter. Beat well and pour in pie shells. Bake at 350° until brown. After 50 minutes, turn oven off and let stand 10 extra minutes.

## Sweet Potato Custard Pie

4 med. sweet potatoes, boiled in jackets (3 cups)  
1 tablespoon vanilla  
½-¾ cup sugar  
1 (5 oz) evaporated milk  
1 stick butter  
4 eggs, separated  
1 tablespoon lemon extract or juice  
2 dashes cinnamon  
2 unbaked pie shells  

Peel potatoes, mash and add butter while potatoes are still hot. Beat egg yolks and add vanilla and lemon. Add sugar to taste. Beat egg whites with the addition of 2 teaspoons sugar until stiff. Turn into pastry shells. Bake at 400° for 10 minutes, then reduce heat to 350° and bake 35 minutes longer or until filling is firm.

## Tropical Pineapple Strawberry Pie

1 cup sugar  
2 cups fresh pineapple  
2 tablespoons rum  
⅓ cup sugar  
¼ cup coconut  
½ cup cornstarch  
1½ pints strawberries  
1 pie shell  
½ cup flour  
⅓ cup margarine  

In large bowl, stir together sugar and cornstarch. Add pineapple, strawberries, and rum. Toss to coat. Put in pie shell. Mix coconut, sugar and flour. Cut in margarine until coarse crumbs form. Sprinkle over pie. Bake at 425° for 15 minutes. Reduce to 350° and bake for 30 minutes longer.

# Cakes, Pies & Cookies

*"The mind forgets, but the heart always remembers"*

# Cookies

### Chocolate Chip Cookies

*Mix together:* **1/3 cup soft shortening, 1/2 cup sugar, 1 egg, 1/3 cup butter, 1/2 cup brown sugar** and **1 teaspoon vanilla.** Set aside.

*Sift together:* **1 1/2 cups flour, 1/2 teaspoon salt** and **1/2 teaspoon soda.** Mix with first batter. Add **1 cup chocolate pieces.** Drop by teaspoonfuls on ungreased cookie sheet. Bake at 325° for 8-9 minutes.

### Potato Chip Cookies

1 cup softened butter  
1/2 cup sugar  
1 3/4 cups flour  

1 teaspoon vanilla  
3/4 cup coarsely crushed potato chips  
2/3 cup confectioners sugar

Mix first five ingredients. Bake at 350° for 10-12 minutes. Let cool for 5-10 minutes. Roll in confectioners sugar. (3 dozen).

**Notes:**

## Sugar Cookies
*(Delicious!)*

1 cup sugar
1 cup vegetable oil

1 cup powdered sugar
1 cup soft margarine

Mix above ingredients and add **2 eggs.** Cream until fluffy, then add **1 teaspoon vanilla, 1 teaspoon soda, 1 teaspoon salt,** and **1 teaspoon cream of tarter.** Mix. Add **4 cups plus 4 tablespoons flour** and **chopped pecans** if desired. Chill. Roll into balls. Press out with bottom of juice glass dipped in sugar. Can use colored sugar. Spray cookie sheet once with Pam.® Bake at 375° for 8-10 minutes.

## The World's Best Cookie

1 cup butter
1 cup brown sugar
1 cup granulated sugar
1 egg
1 cup salad oil
1 teaspoon vanilla
1 cup rolled oats (uncooked)

1 cup crushed corn flakes
1 cup shredded coconut (optional)
½ cup chopped nuts
3½ cups sifted flour
1 teaspoon soda
1 teaspoon salt

Preheat oven to 325°. Cream butter and sugars until fluffy. Add egg and mix well. Add salad oil and vanilla, mixing well. Add oats, corn flakes, coconut (if used), and nuts, stirring well. Add flour, soda and salt. Mix well. Drop by teaspoonfuls onto ungreased baking sheet. Flatten with fork dipped in water. Bake for 12 minutes. Cool on cookie sheet for a few minutes before removing. Makes 8 dozen.

Notes:

# Desserts

*"I'm wishing at this very time that I could but repay a portion of the gladness that you've strewn my way. And if I could have one wish this year, this only would it be — I'd like to be the sort of friend that you have been to me. What a friend we have in Jesus."*

# Desserts

### Baked Apples

8 red apples, cored (do not peel)
½ stick margarine
1 cup sugar

⅛ teaspoon cinnamon
1 box strawberry Jello®

In shallow baking dish, put sliced apple rings. Add butter, sugar and cinnamon. Sprinkle dry Jello® over apples and bake 15 minutes on high in microwave.

### Banana Torte

1 cup graham cracker crumbs
4 tablespoons melted margarine
1 can Eagle Brand® Milk
½ cup lemon juice

2 diced bananas
1 tablespoon sugar
1 cup heavy cream

Combine crumbs and margarine; reserve 2 tablespoons. Press crumbs evenly over bottom of lightly buttered 8-inch square pan. Add ⅓ cup lemon juice to milk. Blend well. Mix bananas and remaining lemon juice and sugar. Fold into milk mixture. Whip cream and fold in. Pour in pan. Sprinkle reserved crumbs on top. Cut into squares.

Notes:

# Desserts

## Bread Pudding

5 slices day-old bread
2 tablespoons butter or margarine
¼ cup moist raisins
¼ teaspoon salt

½ cup sugar
3 eggs
3 cups milk
¼ teaspoon cinnamon

Toast bread in oven. While still warm, butter toast. Arrange toast in baking dish. Sprinkle with raisins. Stir salt and remaining ingredients together. Make 2 layers of bread. Pour half of milk mixture over first layer. Repeat with second layer. Let stand a few minutes until bread soaks well. Sprinkle with cinnamon on top. Bake at 350° for 45 minutes or until knife comes out clean.

## Brownies

1 stick margarine
¼ cup cocoa
¾ cup flour
½ teaspoon baking powder
½ teaspoon salt

2 eggs
1 cup sugar
1 teaspoon vanilla
1 cup chopped nuts

Beat eggs lightly. Add sugar and flour mix. Add vanilla, nuts and melted margarine. Bake in oblong pan (7 x 10) at 350° for 30-35 minutes. Ice with your favorite chocolate frosting. Cool. Cut into squares.

**Notes:**

## Chess Squares

3 cups flour
3 teaspoons baking powder
3 eggs
1½ teaspoons vanilla
½ teaspoon salt

¾ cup margarine
2 cups packed brown sugar
1 cup white sugar
1 cup chopped nuts
1 teaspoon lemon flavoring

Grease jellyroll pan. Melt margarine. Add sugars, eggs, vanilla, flour, salt and baking powder. Mix well. Add nuts. Bake at 350° for 25-30 minutes. Cut while warm.

## Chewies

1 stick margarine, melted
1 box brown sugar
3 eggs
2 cups self-rising flour

1 teaspoon vanilla
1 cup nuts
1 cup coconut

Melt margarine, then stir in sugar and eggs. Add flour and mix well. Fold in vanilla, nuts and coconut. Bake in greased and floured 9x13-inch pan for 40 minutes in a 300° oven.

## Chocolate Sauce

Melt **5 tablespoons margarine**, **⅔ cup evaporated milk** and **2 cups sugar** in microwave. Add **6 oz. chocolate chips** and **1 teaspoon vanilla**. Stir.

**Notes:**

## Cranberry Casserole

3 cups diced unpeeled apples     2 cups raw cranberries

Pour into 9" square Pyrex® dish. Sprinkle with **1 cup granulated sugar** and pour ½ **cup water** over this.

*Topping:*

1 stick melted margarine     1½ cup instant oatmeal
½ cup brown sugar, firmly packed     ⅓ cup flour
½ cup chopped pecans

Mix together and sprinkle the "pastry" topping over cranberries and apples. Bake 1 hour at 350°.

## Creamy Banana Pudding

1 (14 oz.) can Eagle Brand® milk
1 small pkg. vanilla instant pudding mix
36 vanilla wafers
1½ cups cold water

2 cups (1 pt.) whipping cream, whipped
3 med. bananas, sliced and dipped in real lemon juice

In large bowl, combine sweetened condensed milk and water. Add pudding mix. Beat well. Chill 5 minutes. Fold in whipped cream. Spoon 1 cup pudding mixture into 2½ quart glass bowl. Top with ⅓ each of the wafers, bananas, and pudding. Repeat layering twice ending with pudding. Cover. Chill. Garnish as desired. Refrigerate leftovers.

**Notes:**

## Cream Cheese Brownies

| | |
|---|---|
| 1 pkg. Duncan Hines® brownie mix (Family size) | ⅓ cup sugar |
| 2 pkg. (3 oz. each) cream cheese | 5 eggs (total in recipe) |
| 5 tablespoons butter or margarine | 2 tablespoons flour |
| | ¾ teaspoon vanilla |

*Cream cheese mixture.* Soften cream cheese and butter. Beat together. Add sugar, 2 eggs, and set aside.

*Brownie batter.* Empty brownie mix and chocolate flavor packet into medium-sized bowl. Add 2 tablespoons water and 3 eggs. Mix by hand about 50 strokes. Pour half the brownie batter into a greased 9x13-inch pan. Pour all the cream cheese mixture over the brownie layer. Spoon the remaining brownie batter here and there over the cream cheese batter. Pull knife through batter for swirled effect.

Bake at 350° for 35-40 minutes or until done. Cool and frost.

*Frosting:* Melt 3 tablespoons margarine in a medium saucepan. Stir in 2 tablespoons cocoa until dissolved. Add 1½ cups confectioners sugar, 2 tablespoons milk, and 1 teaspoon vanilla. Stir until smooth. Add more milk if necessary. Frost brownies. Set until firm.

## Easy Brownies

| | |
|---|---|
| 1 cup oil | 4 eggs, well-beaten |
| 2 cups sugar | 1 tablespoon vanilla flavoring |
| 1 cup self-rising flour | Dash of salt |

Mix ingredients together. Pour into rectangular shaped, greased and floured pan. Bake at 350° for 20-30 minutes. Cut when cool.

**Notes:**

# Desserts

## Easy Cobbler

½ cup butter or margarine
2 cups sugar
4 cups fresh frozen fruit
    (peaches, strawberries, blackberries, apples)
1 cup self-rising flour
1 cup milk

Melt butter in a 9x13x12-inch pan. Combine flour, 1 cup sugar and milk. Spoon evenly over butter. Do not stir. Combine fruit with remaining cup of sugar (may need more sugar if fruit is tart). Bring to a boil. Ladle over butter. Do not stir. Bake at 375° for 30 to 45 minutes or until brown.

## Jean's Egg Custard

2 eggs
¼ cup plus 2 tablespoons sugar
Dash of salt
1 teaspoon vanilla
1½ cups milk, scalded
1 unbaked pie shell
Nutmeg

Beat eggs. Add sugar, salt and vanilla. Slowly add scaled milk into egg mixture. While blending, pour into pie shell and sprinkle with nutmeg. Bake at 450° for 20 minutes or until slightly shaky.

## Gladys' Egg Custard

Beat **3 eggs** until completely foamy. Add ½ **to** ¾ **cup granulated sugar** and beat until sugar is dissolved. Add **1**¾ **cups whole milk, 1 teaspoon vanilla, dash of nutmeg (optional).** Pour into unbaked pie crust. Bake at 400° for 15 minutes. Turn oven down to 350° and bake until firm.

**Notes:**

## Heavenly Hash

1 (#2) can crushed pineapple
1 med. jar of cherries
½ cup chopped pecans
80 miniature marshmallows
½ pt. whipping cream

Let marshmallows and pineapple soak for about 3 hours, then add cherries, nuts and whipping cream.

## Homemade Ice Cream

1¼ cups sugar
3 eggs, beaten with sugar
1 can evaporated milk
½ gallon milk
⅛ teaspoon salt
2 teaspoons vanilla

Mix above ingredients. Put ice cream in freezer.

*Variations:* 1 (6 oz) can Hershey® syrup, 1 cup crushed pineapple, 4 ripe bananas (mashed), 2 cups strawberries (mashed), 4 ripe peaches (mashed). With fruits, use only 1 teaspoon vanilla.

## Orange Balls

12 oz. pkg. vanilla wafers
1 stick margarine, melted
1 box powdered sugar
1 small can frozen orange juice concentrate

Crush vanilla wafers into crumbs. Add margarine and orange juice mixture. Chill for several hours. Form into small balls and roll in powdered sugar.

**Notes:**

## Mountain Mama's Mudslide

1 stick softened margarine
1½ cups chopped pecans
1 cup confectioner's sugar
2 cups cold milk
1 small pkg. chocolate instant pudding
1 cup flour
4 oz. pkg. cream cheese
1 med. Cool Whip®
1 small pkg. vanilla instant pudding
1 chocolate Hershey® bar

Mix margarine, flour and 1 cup chopped pecans. Press in the bottom of a 9x13-inch pan. Bake at 350° for 20 minutes. Cool completely.

Beat until fluffy, cream cheese and confectioner's sugar. Fold in 1 cup Cool Whip.® Spread over cooled crust. Mix milk, puddings and flour until very thick. Spread over the cream cheese mixture.

Top with remaining Cool Whip.® Grate Hershey® bar over the top. Sprinkle with remaining pecans. Refrigerate overnight or at least 4 hours.

## Pecan Chewies

½ cup margarine (softened)
3 eggs
1 teaspoon vanilla
1 (16 oz) pkg. brown sugar
1½ cups self-rising flour
1 cup chopped pecans

Cream margarine and sugar until light and fluffy. Add eggs, one at a time, beating well after each addition. Add flour, blending well. Stir in vanilla and pecans. Pour into greased pan. Bake at 350° for 30 to 35 minutes. Cut into squares. Serves 30.

Notes:

## Pecan Crispies

½ cup vegetable shortening
½ cup butter
2½ cups brown sugar
2 eggs, beaten
¼ teaspoon salt
½ teaspoon soda
1 cup chopped pecans
2½ cups flour

Thoroughly cream shortening and sugar. Add eggs. Beat well. Add flour, sifted with salt and soda. Add nuts. Drop by teaspoon onto greased cookie sheet. Space about 2 inches apart. Bake in a moderate oven at 350° for 12-15 minutes.

## Pumpkin Roll

3 eggs
1 cup sugar
½ cup solid packed pumpkin
1 teaspoon lemon juice
¾ cup flour
1 teaspoon baking powder
½ teaspoon salt
2 teaspoon cinnamon
½ teaspoon nutmeg or 1½ teaspoons pumpkin pie spice

Beat eggs 5 minutes or until fluffy. Gradually blend in sugar. Stir in pumpkin and lemon juice, then remaining ingredients. Grease and flour jelly roll pan. Spread mixture on pan. Bake 15 minutes at 375° until it comes loose from around the edges. Turn out on dish towel, heavily sprinkled with powdered sugar. Roll up in towel while hot. Leave 1 hour.

*Filling:* Mix 1 cup powdered sugar, 1 (8 oz) pkg. cream cheese, 4 tablespoons soft butter, ½ teaspoon vanilla, and ½ cup chopped nuts (optional). Unroll cake and spread this filling within. Roll back up *without* towel. Wrap in plastic wrap and freeze. Will slice right from freezer.

Notes:

## Puppy Chow

1 stick margarine
1 cup creamy peanut butter
1 (12 oz) pkg. chocolate chips
1 (12.3 oz) box Crispix® cereal (to half recipe, use 6 cups cereal)

Melt together margarine, peanut butter and chocolate chips over low heat. Stir to blend, then pour over the cereal in a mixing bowl. Stir carefully until cereal is evenly coated. Spread out in a 9 x 13" buttered pan. Cut in squares when cooled.

## Snack Treat

1 stick butter
1 cup brown sugar
¼ teaspoon baking soda
6 cups popped corn
2 cups Cheerios®
¼ cup Karo® Syrup
1 teaspoon vanilla
2 cups Rice Chex®
1 cup peanuts
1 cup pretzels (small)

Mix popped corn, Cheerios,® Rice Chex,® peanuts and pretzels. Set aside. Mix butter, Karo® Syrup, sugar and vanilla. Bring to a boil. Boil 5 minutes. Remove from heat and add baking soda. Mix well and pour over dry mixture. Mix well. Spread on cookie sheet. Bake at 200° for 1 hour stirring a couple of times or more.

Notes:

# Candy and Jelly

*"All things are difficult before they are easy"*

## Fudge Candy

5 cups white sugar
1 tall can evaporated milk
1 pt. jar Marshmallow Creme®
2 sticks margarine
3 (6 oz) pkg. chocolate bits
1 cup chopped nuts (optional)

Boil sugar, milk and margarine for 8 minutes. Put chocolate bits and marshmallow creme over this. First stir with spoon. Then use mixer until chocolate bits are melted and fudge is real smooth. Add nuts if desired. *(I use black walnuts or pecans).* Pour into buttered pans.

## Mound Candy Bars

1 can sweetened condensed milk
2 large bags of coconut
1 stick margarine

Mix together. Form into balls. Refrigerate for 30 minutes.

*Chocolate coating:* Melt 2 bags of semi-sweet chocolate chips and $3/4$ block paraffin wax in double boiler. Dip bars in chocolate. Set bars on wax paper to harden.

## Pecan Kisses

1 egg white
Dash of salt
$1/4$ cup sugar
1 teaspoon cinnamon
$1/8$ teaspoon nutmeg
$1/8$ teaspoon cloves
1 cup walnuts or pecans, chopped

Beat egg whites with salt until stiff. Gradually beat in sugar mixed with spices. Fold in nuts. Drop by teaspoonfuls onto a well-greased cookie sheet. Top with halves of nuts. Bake at 250° for 35-40 minutes.

**Notes:**

## Half-Hour Apple Butter

1 (25 oz) jar unsweetened applesauce
½ cup sugar
¼ teaspoon ground allspice
⅛ teaspoon ground cloves
1½ teaspoons ground cinnamon
⅛ teaspoon ground ginger

Combine ingredients in a heavy saucepan, stirring well. Bring to a boil. Reduce heat and simmer, uncovered, for 30 minutes. Stir often. Cool. Pour mixture into container of electric blender. Process at high speed for 10 seconds or until smooth. Store in refrigerator. Yield: 2 cups.

**Notes:**

# Appetizers and Dips

*"To succeed, do the best you can where you are, with what you have"*

## Dips and Spreads

### A Good Dip

1 (8 oz) cream cheese
2 tablespoons onion
Garlic to taste
3 boiled eggs, chopped
½ cup mayonnaise
¼ cup dried parsley
Salt and pepper to taste

Cream cheese and mayonnaise. Add other ingredients.

### Bacon Vegetable Dip

1 pt. sour cream
2 tablespoons lemon juice
4 slices bacon, crisply cooked, drained and crumbled
1 pkg. onion salad dressing mix
½ teaspoon Worcestershire® sauce
½ cup cucumber, finely chopped

Mix and let set in refrigerator at least 1 hour.

### Chipped Beef Dip

2½ oz. jar dried beef
2 tablespoons chopped green pepper
8 oz. cream cheese
8 oz. sour cream
2 tablespoons chopped onion
⅛ teaspoon pepper
2 tablespoons milk
Chopped pecans

Mix ingredients. Top with chopped pecans. Heat at 225° or so for 15 minutes.

Notes:

# Appetizers

### Dill Weed Vegetable Dip

1 cup sour cream
1 cup mayonnaise
2 teaspoon dill weed

1 tablespoon minced onion
1 teaspoon parsley flakes
1 teaspoon seasoned salt

Mix ingredients. Refrigerate for 2 hours. Serve with raw vegetables.

### Deviled Ham Dip

2 (3 oz) pkgs. cream cheese
1/3 cup evaporate milk
2 teaspoon horseradish, drained
2 tablespoons pickle relish

1 teaspoon Worcestershire® sauce
2 teaspoon grated onion or
  1/2 teaspoon onion powder
4 1/2 oz. can of deviled ham

Let cream cheese soften. Add milk, about 2 tablespoons at a time, mixing until smooth each time. Mix in remaining ingredients.

### Dippy Dip

*Melt together and blend:*

1 lb. sharp cheddar cheese
1 1/2 sticks margarine

*Mash together:*

1 can blackeye peas with Jalapeno
2 cans blackeye peas without Jalapeno
1 small can green chiles
1/3 cup onions, diced

Blend the above and serve hot.

**Notes:**

### Egg and Deviled Ham Dip

2 (3 oz) cans deviled ham  
2 eggs, hard cooked and finely chopped  
2 tablespoons finely chopped sweet pickle

Blend all ingredients. Serve with crackers.

### Fabulous Fruit Dip

1 (8 oz) cream cheese  
3 tablespoons powdered sugar  
1 jar marshmallow cream  
1 tablespoon lemon juice

Mix together cream cheese and marshmallow cream. Add sugar and lemon juice. Chill. Serve with fruit.

### Faye's Fruit Dip

1 (8 oz) pkg. cream cheese  
1 ctn. Dannon® plain yogurt  
1½ teaspoons vanilla flavoring  
15 pkgs. Equal® sweetener  
2 teaspoons lemon rind, grated  
1 teaspoon lemon flavoring (optional)

Mix ingredients together until well blended.

**Notes:**

## Hot Beef Dip

1 (8 oz) cream cheese
1 (2½ oz) jar dried beef, chopped
½ cup sour cream

2 tablespoons milk
2 tablespoons onion flakes
¼ teaspoon black pepper

*Topping:*

½ cup chopped pecans
½ teaspoon salt

2 tablespoons butter

Cream together the cream cheese and milk. Add beef, onion flakes, pepper and sour cream. Mix well. Set aside. Melt butter. Add pecans and salt. Put cheese mixture into 6-inch dish and cover with topping. Bake 20 minutes at 350°. **Serve with assorted crackers.**

## Layered Nacho Dip

1 (16 oz) refried beans
1 (8 oz) sour cream
2 tomatoes, diced
1 small onion or 4 green onions, chopped
1½ cups grated Cheddar or Monterey Jack Cheese or half Cheddar and half Monterey Jack

1 (6 oz) avocado dip
1 (4½ oz) ripe olives, chopped or sliced
1 (4 oz) can green chiles, chopped
½ of 1¼ oz. pkg. Taco Seasoning Mix

Combine beans and taco seasoning. Stir well. This is first layer. Next, layer remaining ingredients as listed. Fill in around plate or platter with chips, tortilla or any corn chip. In middle of top, put a few **chopped tomatoes** and a **sprig of parsley.**

**Notes:**

### Rodger's Bar-B-Q Dip (for 1 quart jar)

½ cup sugar  
1½ tablespoons salt  
1½ tablespoons pepper  

Ketchup  
Vinegar  

Combine sugar, salt and pepper. Pour into a quart jar. Add enough ketchup to fill a quart jar, half full. Add enough vinegar to fill jar all but 2 inches from the top. Fill to rim with water. Mix. Use on any kind of meat, grilled or baked.

### Taco Salad Dip

*Mix together:*

1 (8 oz) cream cheese  
1 (8 oz) sour cream  

1 pkg. Taco seasoning mix  

Spread on large plate or platter size of pizza pan. Chill 2 hours or overnight. Then add in layers of the following, just before serving:

2 cups lettuce, chopped  
1 med. onion, chopped  

2 tomatoes, chopped  
1 med. green pepper, chopped  

Serve with **potato chips, nachos, or crackers.**

**Notes:**

# Cheese Appetizers

### Holiday Cheese Ball

1 lb. New York sharp cheese
½ cup chopped pecans

1 (8 oz) pkg. cream cheese
Garlic salt to taste

Grate sharp cheese. Combine with cream cheese. Add garlic salt. Mix in nuts.

### Jean's Cheese Ball

1 (8 oz) cream cheese
1 small can crushed pineapple
  drained
½ cup pecans, chopped fine

1 tablespoon green pepper, chopped
1 tablespoon onion, chopped fine
1 tablespoon seasoning salt

Combine ingredients. Form into ball and roll in 1 cup chopped nuts.

### Jo's Cheese Ball

2 (8 oz) pkgs. cream cheese

1 (10 oz) sharp cheddar cheese

Soften and mix well. Add:

2 tablespoons finely minced onion
2 tablespoons minced green peppers
1 teaspoon fresh lemon juice

2 tablespoons finely minced pimento
2 teaspoons Worcestershire® Sauce

Chill until firm. Shape into ball or long roll. **Roll in chopped pecans.**

Notes:

### Dried Beef Cheese Ball

2 (8 oz) pkgs. cream cheese softened
½ cup creamy Italian dressing
1 small jar dried beef, chopped
Chopped pecans

Mix together cream cheese, dried beef and dressing by hand. Make into a ball. Roll in chopped pecans. Refrigerate for 24 hours before serving.

### Holiday Cheese Ball

2 (8 oz) cream cheese
1 (8½ oz) can crushed pineapple, drained
2 cups chopped pecans
2 tablespoons finely chopped onion
1 tablespoon seasoned salt

Stir 1 cup of pecans, crushed pineapple, onion and salt into softened cheese. Chill until firm. Shape into a ball. Roll in remaining pecans. Serve with favorite crackers. (May add ¼ cup each of red and green pepper for holiday color).

### Nutty Cream Cheese Spread

2 (8 oz) pkgs. cream cheese, softened
1 (4 oz) pkg. ranch-style salad dressing mix
1 (2 oz) pkg. pecan chips
½ cup sour cream

Combine cream cheese, sour cream and salad dressing mix, stir until blended. Chill 10 minutes. Shape mixture into a 6x1-inch patty; lightly coat top and sides with pecans. Serve with crackers.

**Notes:**

# Appetizers

## Pimento Cheese

1½ lbs. sharp cheese
A pinch of sugar
Salt and pepper to taste

3 (4 oz) jars pimento and juice
½ teaspoon vinegar

Mix ingredients.

## Pineapple Au Gratin

1 can chunky pineapple, drained
½ cup sugar
½ stick of margarine

1 cup grated cheese
3 tablespoons flour
Ritz® cracker crumbs

Combine pineapple and grated cheese. Combine sugar with flour. Mix together in shallow dish. Cover top with Ritz® cracker crumbs. Pour margarine over this. Bake at 350° for 30 minutes. (Delicious with ham or pork chops!).

## Pineapple Cheese Ball

2 (8 oz) pkgs. cream cheese, softened
1 (8½ oz) can crushed pineapple, drained
¼ cup finely chopped green pepper

2 tablespoons chopped onion
1 tablespoon seasoned salt
1 cup chopped pecans

Combine cream cheese, pineapple, pepper, onion, and salt. Mix well. Chill. Form mixture into a ball and roll in pecans.

Notes:

## Souper Dooper Cheese Sauce
*"Excellent for fresh vegetables"*

3 tablespoons butter or margarine  
½ teaspoon salt  
1 cup shredded mild cheddar cheese  
¼ cup flour  
1 (13-¾ oz) can chicken broth  
1 teaspoon prepared spicy mustard  

Melt butter and remove from heat. Stir in flour and salt. Slowly stir in broth until mixture is smooth. Return to heat; bring to a boil for 1-2 minutes. Stir in cheese and mustard until cheese melts and sauce is hot. Serve over cooked broccoli, asparagus, or cauliflower.

## Cheese Wafers

½ lb. grated cheese  
¼ lb. butter  
2 cups flour  
Salt, pepper and paprika to taste  
Pecans, whole  

Combine cheese, butter and flour. Season to taste. Divide into 2 parts and roll into balls about 1-inch in diameter. Place a pecan half in the center of each ball. Bake at 375° for 12-15 minutes.

*"Forgiveness is the fragrance that the violet sheds on the heel that has crushed it."*

Notes:

# Pickles

### Dill Pickles

1 qt. vinegar  
2 qts. water  
½ cup salt  
Cucumbers  

1 garlic clove  
1 grape leaf  
1 piece of dill  

Bring all ingredients to a boil. Add scrubbed cucumbers from which stem end has been removed. Let boil until colors change on cucumbers and then place in jars which have already been washed and in which 1 garlic clove, 1 grape leaf, and 1 piece of dill have been added. Pour boiling vinegar over and seal.

### Pickled Beets

1 cup vinegar  
½ cup sugar  
Pickling spices  

2 cups water  
½ teaspoon salt  
Beets  

Cook Beets with skin on until tender. Drain. Pour cold water on and skin them. Cut up. Place in vinegar and bring to boil until hot through. Pack in jars and seal.

### Pickled Eggs

4 cups white vinegar  
2 tablespoons pickling spice  
2 doz. hard-boiled eggs, peeled  

2 teaspoons salt  
½ cup sugar  

Combine ingredients, except eggs. Bring to a rolling boil. Place eggs, in 2-quart jar. Pour hot vinegar mixture over eggs and refrigerate overnight.

Notes:

## Red Heart Pickles

2 gal. cucumbers  
2 cups pickling lime  
3½ cups white vinegar  
1 cup white vinegar  
1 bottle red food color  
2 large bags red heart cinnamon candies  
3½ cups water  
10 cups sugar  
2 gal. water  
1 tablespoon alum  
8 sticks cinnamon  

Peel and cut out seed part of cucumbers equal to 2 gallons in rings (slices ½ inch). Place in a large crock (not aluminum) with 2 cups of pickling lime and 2 gallons of water. Cover and let set for 24 hours.

Remove cucumbers from lime water and rinse until clear. Place cucumbers in ice water (enough to cover) and let set for 3 hours.

Mix 1 cup white vinegar, bottle of food color, and alum. Add liquid to cucumbers. Let simmer for about two hours or until clear. Discard liquid.

Mix 3½ cups water, 3½ cups vinegar, sugar, red heart candies, and cinnamon sticks. Bring to a boil. Pour mixture over cucumber rings. Let set for 24 more hours. Reserve liquid, and place cucumbers in jars. Bring liquid to a boil and pour to fill jars. Seal jars.

## Refrigerator Pickles

7 cups cucumbers, sliced  
1 cup onion, sliced  
1 cup vinegar  
1 cup pepper, sliced  
2 cups sugar  
1 tablespoon celery seed  
1 tablespoon salt  

Mix and put in ½ gallon jar. Keep in refrigerator.

**Notes:**

## Twelve Hour Pickles

1 gal. cucumbers, sliced
½ cup pickling lime
3 tablespoons pickling spice

5 cups vinegar
7 cups sugar

Wash and slice cucumbers. Place in large jar or other *non-metal* container. Cover with water. Sprinkle lime over cucumbers and mix well. Let stand 12 hours.

Take cucumbers out and wash in cold water 4 or 5 times. Combine sugar, vinegar and pickling spice. Dissolve and add cucumbers. Bring to boil and boil for 30 minutes. Put cucumbers and liquid in hot jars and seal.

**Notes:**

# Index

A Good Dip 140
Admonition Coconut Cake 84
Amish Macaroni Salad 37
Amy Gormby's Punch 70
Apple Nut Cake 84
Ardette's Broccoli Casserole 52
Asparagus Casserole 49
Asparagus-Water Chestnut Casserole 49
Autumn Sweet Potato Casserole 62
Bacon Vegetable Dip 140
Baked Apples 126
Baked Beans 30
Baked Cheese Grits 74
Baked Chicken Breast 18
Banana Torte 126
Bar-B-Q Meatballs 5
Barbecue Slaw 33
Barbecued Meatballs 4
Basic Chocolate Cake 85
Bean Salad 37
Beef and Bean Casserole 5
Beef Stew 2
Beef-A-Roni 5
Best Cole Slaw 33
Best Yet Pineapple Cake 87
Betty Jane's Broccoli Casserole 52
Betty Jane's Onion Soup 58
Betty's Chicken Casserole 21
Betty's Cranberry Salad 42
Betty's Fruit Salad 46
Betty's Hospitality Pie 119
Black-Eyed Peas and Sausage 13
Blueberry Nut Crunch 87
Blueberry Salad 45
Boiled Raisin Cake 85

Bread Pudding 127
Breakfast Casserole 13
Brenda's Chicken Casserole 21
Broccoli and Chicken 53
Broccoli and Rice Casserole 54
Broccoli Bake 50
Broccoli Bread 50
Broccoli Casserole of North Carolina 51
Broccoli Cornbread 53
Broccoli Salad 34
Broccoli Soup 54
Brownies 127
Brunch Casserole 14
Budget Casserole 6
Butter Bean Casserole 30
Buttermilk-Chocolate Frosting 86
Buttermilk-Chocolate Pudding Cake 86
Cabbage Casserole 55
Cabbage Rolls 55
Cauliflower and Broccoli Salad 35
Cauliflower Salad 34
Champagne Cake 90
Cheese Wafers 148
Cherry Pound Cake 91
Cherry Pound Cake Frosting 91
Cherry-Orange Salad 45
Chess Cake 91
Chess Squares 128
Chewies 128
Chicken Imperial 22
Chicken Pie 22
Chicken Salad 23
Chicken Spectacular 23
Chicken Supreme 23

Chicken-Asparagus Casserole 19
Chili 6
Chili Beef Soup 7
Chili Sauce (For canning) 7
Chipped Beef Dip 140
Chocolate Chip Cookies 123
Chocolate Chip Pound Cake 92
Chocolate Pie 109
Chocolate Pound Cake 92
Chocolate Sauce 128
Chow Chow 56
Christmas Eve Punch 70
Christmas Rice 74
Claudine's Vegetable Casserole 66
Coconut Cream Pie 110
Coconut Pecan Pie 111
Coconut Praline Pie 111
Congealed Fruit Salad 41
Congealed Salad 41
Copper Pennies 56
Corn Souffle 57
Crab Meat Salad 38
Cranberry Casserole 129
Cream Cheese Brownies 130
Cream Cheese Frosting 89
Creamy Baked Chicken Breasts 24
Creamy Banana Pudding 129
Creamy Praline Pie 112
Creamy Spinach Casserole 63
Creamy Strawberry Punch 70
Crunchy Turkey Casserole 27
Crusty Pound Cake 93

Delicious Chicken Casserole 20
Deluxe Barbecued Meatballs 4
Deluxe Carrot Cake 89
Derby Pie 113
Deviled Ham Dip 141
Diamond Jubilee Applesauce Cake 95
Different Pecan Pie 113
Dill Pickles 149
Dill Weed Vegetable Dip 141
Dippy Dip 141
Donna's Salad 35
Dried Beef Cheese Ball 146
Easy Brownies 130
Easy Chicken Pie 24
Easy Cobbler 131
Egg and Deviled Ham Dip 142
Egg Custard Pie 114
Enchiladas 8
Fabulous Fruit Dip 142
Fast Rolls 75
Faye's Fruit Dip 142
Flossie's 22-Minute Chocolate Cake 83
Flossie's Chicken Casserole 19
Flossie's Chocolate Pie 109
Flossie's Cranberry Casserole 39
Flossie's Fruit Salad 46
Flossie's Thanksgiving Dressing 77
Flossie's Vegetable Casserole 67
Flossie's Zucchini Bread 77
Fresh Coconut Pound Cake 94
Fried Potato Cake 59
Frozen Fruit Salad 46
Fruit Cocktail Cake 95
Fruit Punch 71

Fudge Candy 137
German Chocolate Cream Cheese Cake 96
German Chocolate Upside Down Cake 96
Gladys' Egg Custard 131
Gladys' Sweet Potatoes Casserole 61
Glazed Fruit 47
Good Morning Muffins 75
Grandma's Pumpkin Pie 119
Grandma's Squash Casserole 65
Grated Sweet Potato Yams 59
Green Chili Chicken Casserole 25
Green Pea Salad 36
Half-Hour Apple Butter 138
Ham and Cauliflower Casserole 14
Ham and Cheese Sandwiches 15
Ham and Swiss Cheese Biscuits 15
Hamburger Casserole 8
Hamburger Pie Casserole 9
Hamburger Stuff 9
Heavenly Hash 132
Hilda's Corn Souffle 76
Holiday Cheese Ball 145, 146
Holiday Cranberry Salad 42
Homemade Ice Cream 132
Honeybun Cake 97
Hot Beef Dip 143
Hot Chicken Salad 38
Hot Cran-Apple Cider 71
Hot Mexican Corn Bread 79
Jane's Rice 78
Japanese Fruit Pie 114
Jean's Cheese Ball 145
Jean's Chicken Casserole 20
Jean's Egg Custard 131

Jean's Stuffed Green Peppers 12
Jo's Cheese Ball 145
Juicy Meat Loaf 10
Julie's Black and White Cream Cheese Dessert 120
Junior Johnson's Race Day Biscuits 78
Kath's Broccoli Casserole 51
Kid's Favorite Cadillac Egg Omelet 31
Lasagna 10
Layered Nacho Dip 143
Lemon Chess Pie 114
Lemon Pie 115
Lemon Pound Cake 97
Lemon Supreme Pound Cake 98
Lo's Mixture 64
Macaroni and Tomatoes 14, 78
Marinated Cucumbers and Onions 59
Marinated Slaw 36
Marinated Tomatoes 66
Meatballs 11
Melt In Your Mouth Chicken Pie 25
Mexican Corn Bread 79
Million Dollar Pie 115
Millionaire's Pie 116
Monkey Bread 76
Mound Candy Bars 137
Mountain Mama's Mudslide 133
Mushroom Roast 57
Mushrooms 57
No Bake Lemon Pie 116
No Crust Apple Pie 116
Nut Cake 99
Nutty Cream Cheese Spread 146
Oatmeal Cake 99

Old-Fashioned Apple Pie 117
Old-Fashioned Icebox Fruit Cake 100
Orange Balls 132
Orange Muffins 80
Oven Barbecued Chicken 26
Paradise Island Punch 71
Peach Custard Pie 117
Peach Pie 113
Pecan Cake 100
Pecan Chewies 133
Pecan Crispies 134
Pecan Kisses 137
Pecan Pie 117
Peppered Roast 3
Perfect Pumpkin Pie 118
Perfection Salad 42
Pickled Beets 149
Pickled Eggs 149
Pimento Cheese 147
Pineapple and Strawberry Molds 43
Pineapple Au Gratin 147
Pineapple Cheese Ball 147
Pineapple Pound Cake 101
Pineapple Pound Cake Glaze 101
Pole Winning Pound Cake 103
Poppy Seed Cake 102
Poppy Seed Chicken 26
Portuguese Potato Casserole 60
Potato Casserole 60
Potato Chip Cookies 123
Pound Cake 102
Pretzel Salad 43
Prize-Winning Pumpkin Pie 118
Prune Cake with Buttermilk Icing 103
Pumpkin Roll 134
Punch Bowl Cake 105
Puppy Chow 135
Quick Banana Bread 81
Quick Cheese Grits 80
Raisin Sauce For Ham 16
Red Heart Pickles 150
Red Velvet Pound Cake 104
Red Velvet Pound Cake Frosting 104
Refrigerator Pickles 150
Rodger's Bar-B-Q Dip 144
Salad Dressing 47
Sausage Balls 16
Sausage Casserole 16
Sausage Pinwheels 17
Scotch Apple Pie 121
Scotch Chocolate Cake 105
Seven-Up Salad 40
Shredded Yams 61
Shrimp Marguerite 28
Snack Treat 135
Souper Cooper Cheese Sauce 148
Sour Cream Coffee Cake 106
Sour Cream Pecan Pie 121
Sparkling Fruit Mold 44
Special Occasion Sausage and Eggs 17
Squash Casserole 65
Squash Pie 122
Strawberry Kringle Cake 107
Strawberry-Pretzel Salad 44
Stuffed Mushrooms 58
Stuffed Peppers 11
Stuffed Pork Chops 18
Sugar Cookies 124
Sweet Potato Cake 107
Sweet Potato Casserole with Crunchy Topping 62
Sweet Potato Custard Pie 122
Sweet Potato Souffle 63
Taco Salad Dip 144
Texas Hash 12
The World's Best Cookie 124
Three Bean Casserole 29
Three Bean Hot Dish 29
Toasted Butter Pecan Cake 108
Tropical Chicken Salad 39
Tropical Pineapple Strawberry Pie 122
Tuna Surprise 28
Turkey Tetrazzini 27
Twelve-Hour Pickles 151
Veg-All Casserole 68
Vegetable Casserole 67
Vegetable Salad 36
Wassail Bowl 72
White Wine Cake 88
Whole Wheat Muffins 81
Wilted Lettuce 37
Yellow Squash Casserole 65

# FLOSSIE'S FAVORITES

## ORDER FORM
Allow 6-8 weeks for delivery

Please send me _____ copies of **Flossie's Favorites**     @ $ 14.95 each  
Postage and handling     @ $ 4.00 per book  
Add applicable sales tax     $_____

Total Enclosed     $_____  
(Please do not send cash)

Send your check or money order to:

    Flossie's Favorites  
    c/o Marketing "500" Cookbook  
    Post Office Box 2592  
    Ormond Beach, Florida 32175-2592

**Make all checks payable to:**    Marketing "500" Cookbook

Please Print:

Name _____

Address _____

City _____ State _____ Zip _____

Telephone # ( _____ ) _____